FRANK WORRELL
A Biography

Cricket does not permit a player to masquerade his mistakes behind the success of the team. Cricket is a game that, by its uncertainty, teaches us to accept success and failure with humility.

Sir Frank Worrell

FRANK WORRELL
A Biography

—— ○○○ ——

IVO TENNANT

Foreword by Clive Lloyd
Postscript by Richie Benaud

Lutterworth Press

Cambridge

Lutterworth Press
7 All Saints' Passage
Cambridge CB2 3LS

British Library Cataloguing in Publication Data

Tennant, Ivo
   Frank Worrell: a biography
   1. Worrell, Frank   2. Cricket players —
   Barbados — Biography
   I. Title
   796.35'8'0924   GV915.W66

ISBN 0-7188-2613-2

Designed by Geoff Green
Printed in Great Britain by
St Edmundsbury Press Ltd, Bury St Edmunds, Suffolk

Contents

List of illustrations

Introduction and Acknowledgements

— ooo —

The honest biographer, it was said once, has added a new terror to death. Would Sir Frank Worrell have agreed? A biography is not a biography if it is not honest and my only claim for this book is that I have attempted to portray a great West Indian as honestly as possible. My task, objectivity, has been made easier rather than harder, I think, by being detached from the struggles within the Caribbean.

The subsequent material results from conversations and, in a few cases, correspondence, with more than a hundred people who knew Sir Frank. My research took me to Barbados, Jamaica, Trinidad and Lancashire, and I am grateful to all those who are listed below for their help. Several of the names who will not be identifiable to most readers are old school friends of Sir Frank. I have tried to concentrate in particular on the periods of his life which are least known to the layman: his years in the Lancashire Leagues, his degree course at Manchester University, his period as a Senator and his two years playing for Boys Town in the slums of Kingston; and especially his work for the University of West Indies. If the scorecards of the Test matches in which he played have not been chronicled in great detail, it is because the matches have been well reported elsewhere, most notably in *Wisden*. Sir Frank had a wider view of life than attention to his batting average, which made this book all the more interesting to write.

It struck me when researching it, how much the game of cricket has changed. For instance, Sir Frank never wore a thigh pad, reckoning that the baggy folds of his trousers would cushion being hit by a fast bowler. Try suggesting that to a professional cricketer today. In the 1950s, John Goddard, then captain of West Indies, was suspended from Test cricket for three and a half years for criticisms of the West Indies Board of Control. His lawyer would have a field day if that were to happen now.

The status of cricketers has changed as well. In the 1980s the leading West Indian players occupy an elevated position in Caribbean circles. Men of the stature of Clive Lloyd – who for all his triumphs has not been accorded the adulation that Worrell received – and Vivian Richards confer with West Indian prime ministers and accept what passes for contemporary West Indian wisdom. They are caught up in a more politically aware Caribbean than in Worrell's day. Resentment at the way black cricketers were kept in check by all-white Boards of Control was restrained during Worrell's leadership but surfaced afterwards. In the 1980s it has reached a state of rebellion. The white captains of old such as John Goddard and Jeffrey Stollmeyer are shown little to no respect by some modern-day West Indian players, even though they were Test-class players. One of West Indies' leading fast bowlers of the 1970s and 1980s would snub one of their finest post-war white players when he went into the dressing-room. One reason why Sir Frank was so respected was because he rose above such an outlook, in spite of having suffered from prejudiced thinking himself. The only time he was conscious of his colour was when he looked at himself in the mirror.

The development of the Caribbean has inevitably affected its cricketers. For the young West Indian, there are now more pursuits to follow than was the case when Sir Frank was growing up. For example, football is almost as popular as cricket in some islands. In the 1960s Sir Frank predicted that the leading cricketers would in due course come from the developing islands. He is being proved right.

I would in particular like to thank Gerry Gomez and Brickie Lucas, an old school friend of Sir Frank, for their hospitality in Port of Spain and Bridgetown respectively; Sir Sidney Martin, formerly pro vice-chancellor of the University of West Indies, for supplying considerable detail on Sir Frank's life there; Clive Lloyd, West Indies' other outstanding captain, for writing the foreword and Richie Benaud for writing a postscript; Sir Frank's daughter, Lana, his brother-in-law, Harold Brewster, and one of his closest friends, Noel Symmonds, for considerable help and the last-named for allowing me the use of photographs; Colin Atkin for providing comprehensive details of Sir Frank's career at Radcliffe; Joseph Smith, who followed Sir Frank's career in Lancashire, for his encouragement and recommendations. I should also like to thank Simon O'Hagan, Douglas Rae and Marcus Williams, colleagues at *The Times*, for their suggestions. Not least I wish to thank Mark Peel for the idea of writing this book.

For their help great or small, I thank: Mr Gerry Alexander; Mr Charles Alleyne; Mr Rex Alston; Mr Leslie Ames, CBE; Mr John Arlott, OBE; Mr Denis Atkinson; Mr Trevor Bailey; Mr Alex Bannister; Mr Alec Bedser, CBE; Mr Richie Benaud, OBE; Mr Harold Brewster, CBE; Mr Steve Camacho; Mr Jim Cameron; Mr Bob Cherry, secretary, North Staffordshire and District League; Dr C.B. Clarke; Mr Jim Clarke, secretary, Lancashire Cricket League; Dr Michael Clarke; Mr Ted Dexter; Mr Maurice Foster; Mr Lance Gibbs; Mr Stanton

Gittens; Mr John Goddard; Mr Gerry Gomez; Mr Billy Griffith, DFC, OBE; Mr Charlie Griffith; Mr Bagenal Harvey; Mr Jackie Hendriks; Mr Edward Hoad; Mr David Holford; Mr J.K. Holt jun.; Mr Conrad Hunte; Sir Leonard Hutton; Mr C.L.R. James; Mr Hines Johnson; Mr Rohan Kanhai; Mr Edwin Kay; Mr John Kay; Mr Esmond Kentish; Mr Donald Lacy; Mr Jim Laker; Mr Peter Lashley; Mr Vic Lewis; Mr Clive Lloyd; Mr Brickie Lucas; Mr Trevor McDonald; Mr Easton McMorris; Mr Lester Meredith, secretary, North Staffordshire League; Mr George Mudie; Mr Deryck Murray; Mr Lance Murray; Mr Bob Normandale; Mr Tom Peirce, CBE; Professor Emrys Peters; Mr J.C. Proute; Mr Allan Rae; Mr Sonny Ramadhin; Mr Strebor Roberts; Mr Fred Rogers; Mr D.J. Rutnagur; Mr Reg Scarlett; Mr Brian Scovell; Mr Harry Sealy; The Hon. the Revd Dr Hugh Sherlock, OJ, OBE, JP; Mr Cammie Smith; Mr Joseph Smith; Sir Garfield Sobers; Mr Ivo de Souza; Mr Brian Statham, CBE; Mr Jeffrey Stollmeyer; Mr Algie Symmonds, GCM; Mr Macdonald Symmonds; Mr Noel Symmonds; Mrs Lana Swaby; Mr E.W. Swanton, OBE; Mr Frank Taylor; Mr Bob Taylor; Mr Arthur Thomas; Mr Clyde Walcott; Mr Chester Watson; Mr Kenneth Warren; Mr Cecil Williams; Mr 'Foffie' Williams; Mr Harold Wolfe; Mr John Woodcock. From Radcliffe CC I thank Mr Dan Battersby; Mr Bob Cooper; Mrs Billy Greenhalgh; Mr Martin Greenhalgh; Mr Jack Rigg; Mr John Schofield. I thank Mr Edley Deans, OD, Clerk to the Houses of Parliament, Jamaica and Mr H. Kulkrini, research officer librarian to the Houses of Parliament. From the University of West Indies I thank Mr Lloyd Braithwaite; Mr Selwyn Griffith; Mr Carl Jackman; Sir Arthur Lewis; Sir Sidney Martin; Professor Gladstone Mills; Mr Baldwin Mootoo. I am grateful also to have had the use of the libraries of *The Times*, the *Daily Telegraph*, *The Gleaner* and *Staffordshire Sentinel* newspapers, and the photographic library of *The*

Times. For their assistance I thank also the BBC; the faculty of economic and social studies, Manchester University; the librarians of the public library in Bridgetown and the Central Westminster reference library.

C.L.R. James read the chapter on captaincy, John Schofield, formerly captain of Radcliffe, read the chapter on Radcliffe and Harold Brewster read the entire text.

I would mention that for uniformity throughout the book I have referred to Sir Frank by his surname and his wife and daughter by their christian names.

Foreword by Clive Lloyd

I deem it an honour to be asked to write the foreword to this biography of Sir Frank Worrell.

Sir Frank will be remembered for his wonderful service to West Indies cricket. He was a magnificent player – as elegant a batsman as ever walked to the wicket and by any standards a very reliable bowler. He will be remembered by all for serene leadership and as someone who commanded loyalty and respect from his players. They in return had an affection for him to the extent that many people thought he had special powers.

It was one of the disappointments of my life that I did not have the pleasure of playing under him. I am sure our cricket was the poorer when he passed away. If ever there was a man to bring the West Indies nation closer together it was Sir Frank. He was a person of vision. I remember him saying in 1966 in Antigua, when asked about the future of West Indies cricket, that if the standard was to be maintained, West Indies would have to look to the Leeward and Windward Islands for their future players. This was because industrialisation in Trinidad and Jamaica was having a serious effect on our talents. Looking back at

West Indies teams of the last twelve years, it is clear that Sir Frank was absolutely spot on. We will never know what more this great man would have achieved.

When I was made captain of the West Indies team way back in 1974, I considered my term to be an extension of what Sir Frank started. I sincerely hope I have done him proud. I am sure this book will give one and all an insight into a great West Indian who was not only one of our best captains but a respected and proud ambassador for the West Indies nation. Last but not least, he was a gentleman who won the hearts of most people he met through his charming personality.

April 1986

1
The comity of nations

—— ○ ○ ○ ——

As long ago as the start of the twentieth century it was axiomatic that once the cricketing talent in West Indies was properly developed and directed, the nation could become as competent as England, who gave them the game, or Australia. In the last decade that expectation has been exceeded, to the point of their dominance that we know today. To say that this was the work of one man would be untrue, but one man did make it possible. Sir Frank Worrell paved the way for others to follow.

He was the first black man regularly to captain West Indies and, for the sake of his own race, he could not afford to fail. He succeeded not merely on the field of play, showing that a black man could be as good a leader – and in his case a better leader – than the white men who had gone before. He managed to unite hitherto self-interested cricketers from a scattered group of islands with differing culture and history, separately governed. He expanded the conception of West Indians and cultivated the image of the black man around the world.

The sense of self takes time to expand. It took several years for Worrell to develop from a self-centred youth to a person whom the Vice-Chancellor of the University of West Indies was moved to describe as the embodiment of excellence for West Indians. He was not a paragon of virtue but by then his causes and goals outshone self-seeking: that alone was evidence of his maturity. He was an outstanding cricketer born with a natural talent for games whereas his effectiveness as a leader was commensurate with the growth of his personality. The arrogance of his youth and his somewhat lazy and carefree existence had by then been supplanted by a stress on the virtues of discipline, hard work and pride in oneself and one's country. Excelling at leadership was ultimately of far greater importance, both to himself and to his country, than his achievements as a batsman or bowler.

Gaining a degree as a mature student gave Worrell a status in the 1950s without which, as a black professional cricketer, he would probably not have captained West Indies. His degree led to his participation in other ways in the Caribbean's development at a time when it was seeking independence. As a Hall Warden and then a Dean of Students within the University of West Indies, itself feeling its way, he would not countenance parochialism: the well-being of the University always came first. He became a Senator in Jamaica, a worker in sociology with the Government of Trinidad and was offered the Governor-Generalship of Barbados by its Prime Minister. At the time of his death he could have taken almost any job in the Caribbean he desired.

Worrell died at the age of 42, from a virulent blood disorder. He was a fatalist, and said he would not live long. He was the first sportsman to be given a memorial service at Westminster Abbey. Today his name is revered as perhaps no other West Indian's is. His early death enhanced his celebrity. What would he have done with the second half of his life? Many are still pondering upon it.

2
Beginnings in Barbados

—— ○○○ ——

Frank Mortimer Worrell was born on 1 August 1924, the middle child of a steward in the Merchant Service. It was not, as he said himself, the most likely appellation for a cricketer – and in time he changed his second name to 'McGlinne'. In other ways, appropriate for a man who developed fatalistic beliefs, his future was predetermined.

He was born and grew up in a house overlooking a cricket ground in Barbados, the tiny pear-shaped island at the southernmost end of the Caribbean archipelago. It was a British island, and remained so until a year before his death. It was conservative, insular and a democracy: not for nothing known as 'Little England'. Being British, it was a cricketing island. The game was probably first played there in the eighteenth century. Nowhere in the world is there a more concentrated area of enthusiasm and skill for cricket than within these 166 square miles. The inter-colonial tournament (now Shell Shield) was started in Barbados and the island itself dominated it. Indeed, it won seven of the twelve tournaments staged before the First World War.

Barbados also performed well against English touring

teams. A.W.F. Somerset, who led two MCC sides in the Caribbean after the turn of the century, felt they were more difficult to beat than a West Indian XI, so well did they play together. The solid British middle-class, the colonials, kept the talented but volatile natives on a tight rein at club and inter-colonial level. 'Puritanism incarnate', C.L.R. James called it.

Insularity, then, also pervaded the cricket field. It was not surprising. Caribbean islands are in some cases hundreds of miles apart. Jamaica, for example, is 1500 miles distant from Barbados. Welding together individuals from differing backgrounds and islands proved to be beyond the realm of colonialism.

Into this narrow but stable world were born within eighteen months and a mile or so, Frank Worrell, Clyde Walcott and Everton Weekes. They were to become known, inevitably once of national fame, as the 'three "W"s'. As boys, Worrell and Walcott, growing up in middle-class Bajan families, did not mix with Weekes, who came from a poor background in a district of Bridgetown, the capital. None would have socialised much outside of school with the whites, who comprised a small percentage of the population. The boundaries were clearly defined along the lines of the British class system.

Worrell was raised in Pavilion Road, a mile outside the urban sprawl of Bridgetown. The detached, three-bedroomed house still stands, although a large corrugated iron fence (the old smaller one was blown down by a hurricane) now obliterates the view of Empire Cricket Club, which in Worrell's youth was the strongest on the island. Worrell was brought up not by his parents but by his grandparents, or to be accurate, his grandmother, Florence Burrows. His father, Athelstan, was rarely at home and was to emigrate like so many West Indians to the United States. In the 1920s and 1930s the States promised a wider range of jobs, better pay and status. Even inter-colonial cricketers left. The young George Headley was saved for cricket only because there was confusion over his papers.

Worrell was the sole member of his family not to emigrate: it meant a lonely childhood, even though he made friends easily. Later, he was deterred from joining his family owing to the relative lack of cricket in the States. His brother, Livingstone, four years older and something of a comical character, went with Worrell's father and became an electrician; at the time of writing he is still alive and living in Newburgh. His sister, Grace, went with them and in time married and stayed; she, too, is still alive. Worrell's mother, also named Grace, left as well.

Had Worrell not been at elementary school when they departed, it is probable that he would have joined the exodus and not advanced his cricket career beyond the West Indian XI in Brooklyn, for which his brother played. As it was, his passion for the game grew by the day in Barbados: he would sit atop the family home munching his grandmother's sugar cane and absorbing the club cricket of the day. He started to play the game when he was six. At his elementary school, Roebuck, which he attended from 1930 to 1937, and where the motto is 'manners maketh man', he was one of only two boys to own a bicycle – an indication that the family's finances were healthier than some. Worrell's clothes were sent from the States, not that he appreciated them at the time. His friend, Harold Brewster, later to become his brother-in-law, recalls 'a most untidy schoolboy, shirt-tail out, one sock on and always laughing'. His grandmother, a kind, homely person, was strict, but Worrell usually found a way round her.

There was no playground at Roebuck so with the other boys from Bank Hall – the district in which his home was situated – Worrell would repair to Empire after school and help the groundsman pull the roller in return for which they would be permitted to play with a bit of wood and a composition ball on the outfield. Worrell showed an early aptitude for games, most particularly football. So, too, unknown to him, did Everton Weekes. Later, both concentrated on cricket owing to the risk of injury and because cricket was the premier game in Barbados. It was a decision made with regret. After he had retired from first-class cricket, Worrell said he felt football offered greater enjoyment than cricket, both to players and spectators.

It was when Worrell went to secondary school that his games playing abilities were given shape. Combermere School was renowned for its sporting achievement and had a reasonable scholastic reputation. It was a leading secondary school on the island, State-run but charging eight dollars a term which went up to twelve when the pupil reached the third form. (In 1937 this was a sum of money beyond the pockets of many Barbadians. Later, it waived fees as did the other schools which charged.) Combermere's masters were dedicated. They included in their number Derek Sealy, then one of the finest cricketers in the Caribbean, who played for West Indies eleven times. He was quick to spot Worrell's talents. A month after Worrell joined the school, he was in the 1st XI, although he would rather have been with his Bank Hall chums. It was resented. Worrell, whose natural gait throughout his life was with his head held high, was labelled 'a big-head'.

On his first appearance for the 1st XI, captained by Brewster, he walked to the wicket in short trousers, or pants as they were called, just as Sealy had done on his debut for Barbados. Then, Sealy made a century; now, his protege was less successful. Against a club named Police, Worrell scored 19 and 0, and, bowling slowly, took three wickets for 69. The nickname of 'petit garcon' was then added to that of 'typoo' (he could not pronounce the 'f' in the brand name of a tea). He kept his place in the team, batting at number eleven and continuing to take wickets.

The school teams in Barbados, which played first-class cricket against the island's clubs, were made up of both boys and masters. In *Cricket Punch*, Worrell wrote: 'It was a bit tough for a thirteen year-old boy to be playing in top-grade cricket. Nevertheless, it was a great experience. I found myself up against some of the best players in West Indies and there is no better way of learning anything than by coming up against the finest exponents'.

Within the school, Worrell fared less well. Stanton Gittens, an assistant master, remembers 'a brighter than average pupil who was not particularly industrious'. He played truant and was given a fearful dressing-down by another master for telling a lie: it coloured Worrell's attitude to honesty for the rest of his life. Masters as well as boys continued to resent his prowess on the field. His housemaster told him off for not getting out and giving others a chance to bat in a house match. The headmaster, the Revd Arthur Armstrong, lectured him in front of the school, tired of complaints about him. Worrell felt it to be the worst moment of his life. He was even suspended from cricket and given six lashes by a master, Ralph Perkins, when caught slipping out to the local cinema. On another occasion he was replaced in the 1st XI by his friend, Leroy Critchlowe, another left-arm spinner, after not paying his subscription – an error caused by negligence rather than a lack of money. Worrell wrote later that he suffered at school from a persecution complex.

> Those were the days when child psychology was not a subject demanded of applicants to teachers' posts. Indeed, the majority of masters did not have the experience of raising families of their own. There was no allowance for the original point of view.

However, Worrell matriculated in the Cambridge School Certificate, joined the scouts, sang in the church choir, tolerated athletics, played table-tennis at the YMCA, and at the age of eighteen represented Barbados as a forward at football. At the same age, when still at Combermere – it

was his decision to stay on – he made his debut for the
island at cricket. Also making his first appearance was a
youth with notably wide shoulders who meted out fearful
treatment to bowlers. Clyde Walcott had played with
Worrell at Combermere, where they did not get on particularly well. They were to start together at Test level,
too, by when they had been joined by the poor relation,
Everton Weekes.

3
Exploratory years

— ○ ○ ○ —

At Combermere Worrell had been regarded as a promising
left-arm orthodox spinner, one who could put the ball on a
length and turn it at the age of nine, but of lesser ability as
a right-hand batsman. He was, although he wore his watch
on his right hand, naturally right-handed. Until he was
seventeen his size and lack of strength constricted his range
of shots. Consequently, blessed with good eyesight and a
natural eye for the ball, his stance being based on that of
Leroy Critchlowe's brother, Eric, the runs he scored were
mostly behind the wicket. He took a great delight in late
cutting, as he did throughout his career. There were times
when he seemed to cut the ball almost out of the wicket-
keeper's gloves. He could not, though, cope with the high
bouncing ball, becoming tucked up against it, and this too
stayed with him at higher levels.

By 1942, his last year at school, Worrell had had five
years experience of first-class cricket. In his debut for
Barbados against Trinidad during an inter-colonial tournament affected by the Second World War, he was sent in
last, and in the return match, tenth. He made 70 runs in
four innings with a top score of 34 not out. A family friend

presented Worrell with a bat after his first innings. As for his bowling, for which he had been chosen, he was not successful.

Worrell's cricket master, Derek Sealy, was also in the side, which was captained by Tom Peirce. Worrell was fortunate in his first captain. During the two matches in Trinidad, another white Bajan came to the Barbados dressing-room and suggested to Peirce that he bring some of the white cricketers round for drinks. Peirce responded: 'I bring both blacks and whites or none at all'. It naturally gained him the respect of black cricketers, Worrell not least.

Barbados returned to Trinidad the following year, Worrell again being selected. He went, as before, as a bowler, and suffered at the hands of those two famed Trinidadians, Jeffrey Stollmeyer and Gerry Gomez. Trinidad declared at 449 for nine and won comfortably, but not before Worrell had made an impact with the bat, going in as nightwatchman and finishing with an undefeated 64. For the second match he was moved up the order – to number four. He took his chance. Against an attack that included Gomez and the fast bowlers Lance Pierre and Prior Jones, with whom Worrell was to become firm friends, he made 188, his maiden first-class century.

The score itself was indicative of emerging talent but it was the manner in which the runs were made which caught the eye. There was scant trace of nerves or anything other than textbook strokes. Indeed, during those matches Worrell would sometimes remark that a certain shot was 'too risky'. His runs on the matting came against speed and spin alike, the ball elegantly dispatched, the feet quickly into position. In the second innings he made 68. The match was drawn but Worrell, on his return to Barbados, was feted. When he entered The Empire cinema with his friend, Noel Symmonds, those already seated stood up and cheered.

For the remainder of the war, Worrell's first-class cricket was limited almost entirely to a few matches against Trinidad. In a quest to find another vocation, and some remuneration, he joined the Combermere staff and taught general subjects. It was not, he swiftly discovered, the career for him. Further, he was still suffering from a persecution complex. There was something in it: he was not popular in so far as he had not been popular at school. On an island the size of Barbados he felt fettered every step he took.

So, with no family ties to keep him, Worrell took wing to Trinidad where he had been well received. He stayed but a month, for neither the matting pitches nor the beaches, such as there were, were to his liking. The only bathing of note was on the north coast, a long drive from the capital and cricket centre, Port of Spain. So back to Bridgetown he came, the first of several homecomings. Worrell took a job at the Demerara Life insurance company but that, too, turned out to be a false start. He left before a year was out, being too well-mannered for the exacting task of selling policies and unable to hit it off with his boss, Natty Layne, who thought Worrell was taking custom from him.

On the cricket field, he continued to make progress. He joined Empire and equalled 'Foffie' Williams' record score for the club, 201. When he reached it he gave his wicket away. He was again selected for Barbados in 1944, when Trinidad made a return visit. Before a critical crowd at Kensington Oval, keen to see whether his runs in Port of Spain had been a deception, Worrell struggled with the bat but for the first time at this level showed his potential with the ball. He helped bowl Barbados to victory with match figures of nine for 64. In the second encounter he achieved even more: having toiled in the field while Stollmeyer made 210 and Trinidad 490 for eight, Worrell went in to bat on the second afternoon, joining John Goddard at the crease.

The pitch, as with so many in Barbados, was perfect for batting, blunting the thrust of Pierre and Jones. Goddard, left-handed and full of determination, fastened onto anything short while Worrell elegantly drove what was over-pitched. He outscored his experienced partner, reaching his first century in Barbados for which he was presented with a chicken by a spectator. On and on the pair went, making cricketing history. For the first time in inter-colonial cricket two batsmen were at the crease throughout a day's play. When Barbados finally declared on the fourth morning, Worrell had reached 308 and Goddard 218. Their fourth wicket partnership realised 502, being the third highest for any wicket in first-class cricket. It was to be Worrell's highest score in his career.

Rapturous was the acclaim, and rightly so. There was another significance. The stand represented old and new Barbados: Goddard a leading businessman who was to become one of the last white captains of West Indies; Worrell one of a generation which implemented change. The two respected each other and were united in purpose, at least on the cricket field.

4
Escape

— ○ ○ ○ —

Sir George Headley, a distant cousin of Worrell, would tell of an experience he suffered in 1939, whilst being ferried with other Jamaican cricketers across the Caribbean. He had by then made his name, and was to captain West Indies, the first black man to do so other than Constantine deputising for a short period during one Test. Yet on this crossing Headley was allocated sleeping quarters by the engine room. The white players dined at the captain's table and were allotted better berths. Two maintained on their passports that they were white when in reality they were only slightly fairer than black.

Headley tolerated it: Worrell would not have done. As his status as a cricketer grew, so too did his reputation for standing up for himself – and others. He questioned lines of demarcation within the Barbados team and why he was not permitted to practise at Kensington Oval when white cricketers were. He could not accept that there were no blacks working in the Barbados' banks or that a man of the calibre of Grantley Adams (later Prime Minister of Barbados) could not belong to the yacht club on account of the colour of his skin. Although never a racialist himself,

Worrell would say that a Bajan accent jarred in a white man's voice. As a middle-class black in a country where cricket was solely an amateur sport, the only job options he felt to be open to him were teaching, for which he was unsuited, and the Civil Service. He walked the length of Bridgetown's Broad Street and was unable to find anything gainful.

There was a theory that Worrell disliked over-exposure in a narrow environment, that he was too shy to walk down the main streets of Bridgetown, knowing he would be recognised. He felt he would be more suited to Jamaica, a bigger island, a wider society with more job opportunities, miles distant from Barbados. Although he had been seeing a great deal of one of Harold Brewster's sisters, Velda, the second of nine children of a photographer, he had taken to Jamaican girls who were less inhibited.

The war had ended and inter-colonial cricket had resumed in Jamaica as it had in British Guiana. Worrell would have no difficulty finding a club: in the 1945–6 season he had furthered his reputation by beating, in partnership with Walcott, the record he had achieved with Goddard. In another match in Trinidad, the only inter-colonial encounter that season, they put on an unbroken 574, beating Sutcliffe and Holmes' score of 555 for any wicket made in 1932. Walcott made 314, Worrell 255, their occupation of the crease lasting five hours 41 minutes. Between overs they would set targets, in the manner of experienced batsmen.

Worrell was recognised as one of the best batsmen in Barbados. He was welcomed in Jamaica by Headley's club, Kensington, and played alongside him at Senior Cup level. He found employment, firstly in King Street, Kingston, working at the Government statistics office, and later as a PRO for Reynolds' aluminium firm near Ocho Rios. He set up home in Windward Road on the outskirts of Kingston with a friend named Dusty Richards, who ran a taxi business. He then moved down the road to live in the spacious home of Rual Vaz, whom Worrell referred to as his adopted godfather.

Vaz' outlook on life had a considerable influence on Worrell. He was a philanthropist Jamaican, comfortably off through running his own transport company and owning a cinema. He was not a cricketer but was president of Lucas (Headley's former club) and gave financial help to players in need. He met the expenses of Hines Johnson, the fast bowler, on West Indies 1950 tour to England. Vaz met Worrell through watching him play, and at his home introduced him to various of his friends.

Some of them would accompany Worrell on moonlight picnics on Fridays and Saturdays. Soon, so many were being organised that whether or not the moon was out ceased to be a consideration. At other times Worrell would go to the cinema, play tennis and he swam most mornings at Bournemouth Baths in Kingston. He would visit friends at the University College of West Indies, not far from his home, and ask them what he should read to widen his outlook. He played inside-left at football, at which he had no little talent, for a Jamaica Awards XI against a combined schools team.

So Worrell was ready, mentally as well as physically, for MCC's 1948 tour. He had made runs for Barbados, the island he was pleased to have left, and was starting to impress playing for Jamaica. His technique was compact and correct, particularly as West Indian techniques go. He timed the ball well, using a lot of left hand. The late cut was as much in evidence as in his schooldays. Walcott especially admired his effective on-drive, never hit hard. Worrell had benefitted, too, from two short exhibition tours of New York, one of which was led by Headley.

MCC sent a weakened side under Gubby Allen's captaincy. There was no Bedser, Compton, Edrich, Hutton, Wright or Yardley, although a spate of injuries necessitated a call being made to Hutton to join the party. They did not win once, all seven island matches being drawn and West Indies winning two of the four Tests. Worrell, because of his high-scoring for Barbados, was selected for the first Test but had to stand down through suffering from food poisoning. Headley was appointed to captain West Indies but was then injured and did not play again in the series. Gerry Gomez was captain for the second Test in his native Trinidad and Goddard led for the remainder of the series.

The first Test was drawn, West Indies having the better of it. Worrell recovered in time to make his debut at Port of Spain; this was likewise Walcott's Test debut. England made 362, of which Billy Griffith scored 140 before being leg-before to Worrell – his sole wicket in the series, which illustrated that his bowling had not developed as expected. It was, Griffith remembers, a dubious decision. As Griffith walked back past the bowler, less perturbed than he might have been in the knowledge that he had a hundred to his name, Worrell said to him: 'Billy, I hope you don't think I appealed for that'.

In West Indies' first innings of 497 Worrell, batting at number four, made 97, adding 100 for the fifth wicket with Gomez. It took him three and a quarter hours, contained a six and nine fours and impressed all who saw it. Worrell did, though, blot his copybook during the match. He asked Gomez, his captain, if he could be substituted whilst he went to the airport to meet his sister. Gomez naturally refused. 'It was a silly and arrogant request', said Gomez. 'Fortunately in those days superstars could be handled.'

The second Test was also drawn, but West Indies won the third, in Georgetown. They were rescued from a poor start by Worrell who, batting at number five, duly scored his maiden Test century. *Wisden* recorded that 'he was always master of the situation. He used his reach to good effect'. When Goddard declared, he was on 131, having given no semblance of a chance in three hours thirty-five minutes and having struck fifteen fours. On a turning pitch England were bowled out twice and West Indies won by seven wickets, Worrell not being required to bat again.

Next, Worrell carried his bat for 106 playing for Jamaica against MCC at Melbourne Park – one of the two centuries he scored for his adopted island. The last Test, played at Sabina Park, was also won by West Indies, this time by ten wickets. Weekes scored his maiden Test hundred, the first of five consecutively, and Worrell made 38 out of West Indies' first innings of 490. England were largely unable to cope with the hostility of Johnson, who returned an aggregate of ten for 96.

So it had been a memorable start for Worrell. In four Test innings, two of them not out, he had scored 294 runs at an average of 147, heading the averages of a winning team. It had been a tour untouched by controversy. Yet Worrell decided on a change. He wrote in *Cricket Punch*: 'I wanted to get right away from the West Indies to a place where they didn't know me, where there would be no bitter memories of canings for imaginary offences, no sneers about my conceit'. It was only later, when he had left West Indies, that Worrell realised his worries about his schooldays were but a figment of his imagination. Any ill-feeling towards him that carried over was as a result of his decision to quit Barbados. He was to be booed when he returned, even after being made captain of West Indies.

5
Radcliffe

— ○ ○ ○ —

If to become an inter-colonial cricketer was an ambition in itself for a West Indian, to become a League professional in England was to take it a step further. Learie Constantine had paved the way and had been followed by the likes of Ellis Achong and Manny Martindale. The postwar years, before local industry in Lancashire contracted and before the county clubs creamed off the talent at a younger age, was a propitious time.

Constantine had made a name for himself at Nelson, a Lancashire cotton town which lay north of Radcliffe, Worrell's club to be. One was in the Lancashire League, the other in the Central Lancashire League (the two Leagues are often confused). Each was permitted to field one professional whose duties, not arduous, would comprise playing at the weekend and coaching plus the occasional game in the week. Worrell knew of Constantine's exploits in England, but he knew nothing of Radcliffe. He had not heard, either, that during his inaugural Test series he had impressed their president, Arthur Hampson, who had been on a cruise in the Caribbean. Hampson sent a telegram to Jack Lowe, a textiles trader who, although not

1 Radcliffe, 1952. Back (left to right): Worrell, Baxter, Schofield, Dearden, Berry, Fletcher. Front (left to right): Lord, Stansfield, Greenhalgh (captain), Hamilton, Hoyle.

2 West Indies touring team to England, 1963. Back (left to right): Duckworth (scorer), Butcher, Carew, King, White, Griffith, Gibbs, Nurse, McMorris, Pye (masseur). Middle (left to right): Gaskin (manager), Rodriguez, Kanhai, Valentine, Worrell (captain), Hunte (vice-captain), Sobers, Hall, Burnett (assistant manager). Front (left to right): Murray, Allan, Solomon. (Photo: S & G Press Agency)

3 The youthful Worrell drives off the back foot, all poise and elegance.

a sportsman, was a benefactor of Radcliffe who had been scouring *Wisden* in an attempt to discover a likely professional. A telephone call to John Ikin, who had been in MCC's party in West Indies, confirmed the impression of a young man with all-round ability and a crowd-pleasing style. Ikin replied: 'I am sure Worrell could do a great job in the Leagues and believe he would be interested in furthering his cricketing education by gaining experience of English conditions.' Lowe, on Radcliffe's behalf, engaged Worrell on a salary of £500 for the 1948 season, with an option for a second year. After two seasons this was upped to £700. It was a good wage (paid in part by Lowe) and there were perks: free air fares and accommodation, and match collections. For taking five for 30 or fewer runs, or scoring a half-century, the bucket would go round. Often £50–£60 would be handed to the fortunate player. Worrell appreciated this and had a leather collection bag specially made for him. One month he was enriched by £96.

Worrell's presence would, of course, swell the gate. On occasion 4,000 would pack the small town's cramped ground. To have an international cricketer on the doorstep was still a rarity; this was before the days of television, when transport was restricted. An outing to Manchester, some ten miles distant, was not a common occurrence. There was, then, a greater sense of belonging in working-class communities, and the nature of life in the North was to put a premium on the immediate taking of pleasures. League cricket was a prime entertainment.

In Worrell's first years in England he lived for the present, as is the West Indian way. Neither he nor his fiancée, as Velda was when they came to Radcliffe, were hoarders. 'We've made our money in England and we'll spend it in England,' she once told Bob Cooper, a Radcliffe supporter. In time the Worrells were able to move from the modest house with an outside lavatory that Radcliffe provided in Ulundi Street and buy their own house, a semi-detached on the Bury and Bolton Road in neighbouring Ainsworth. They married at St Andrews Church, Radcliffe, in May 1948 and the following year Velda gave birth to a daughter, whom they named Lana. Lowe and another Radcliffe friend, Jack Plant, were her god-fathers. She was their only child, Velda having a miscarriage two years later.

Worrell's colleagues, unfamiliar with West Indians, were initially somewhat confused by his quiet demeanour. Their recollections are of a shy young man dressed in a brown suit and possessing little else other than his cricket boots. He would let his hair down only with Walcott and Weekes, then League cricketers elsewhere. 'There would be a number of beer bottles outside his door when we put our milk bottles out,' recalled his team-mate, John Schofield. Worrell once wore a badge proclaiming 'champion beer drinker'.

It took the Worrells, particularly Velda, six months to come to terms with the English climate. 'We spent more time under the blankets than outside,' her husband admitted. But both of them came to love the country as Worrell began to make his mark on the field. Although standards in the League were higher than in the 1980s, a gulf separated Worrell from the amateurs. He made a duck on his first appearance – how often this happens to a top-flight batsman – but soon no one could dispute his class. Having got the measure of the slow north country pitches on which the ball was not standing up to be driven as in the Caribbean (but which would be doctored to suit the professional) the runs flowed. Dan Battersby, another Radcliffe colleague, cites one of Worrell's early innings in League cricket in support of his estimation that even on bad pitches his batting was 'poetic'. 'Frank', said Battersby, 'made an undefeated century by scoring all his runs along the ground and mostly in front of the wicket. We learned much just by watching him'.

They learned, too, that Worrell was uninhibited. He would plant his left leg down the pitch and, with his right knee on the ground, hit the ball past the bowler with a straight bat. His party piece was to late cut a ball on middle stump with the back of the bat. But he never humiliated an amateur. He made, that first season, 773 runs in 22 innings at an average of 51.53 – a good start although he came only third in Radcliffe's averages – and bowling medium-pace or slow took 58 wickets at 13.12 apiece. The following season he set a League record, scoring 1501 runs at 88.29 with six centuries. He topped the averages. Three years later, the season after West Indies successful tour of England, Worrell broke his own aggregate. He scored 1694 runs at 112.93, a record aggregate and average for the Central Lancashire League which still stands, even though two more clubs joined after his time. He would doubtless have made more runs but for the weather preventing him from playing three innings on the last four Saturdays of the season. Not surprisingly there are those who, when taking solely batting into consideration, would have him in their side before another of Radcliffe's professionals – Gary Sobers.

Not even Sobers could overtake another record which Worrell helped set up in 1952. Billy Greenhalgh, Worrell's regular opening partner, put on 303 in four hours with him for the first wicket against Middleton. The attack included their professional, Eric Price, a former Lancashire and Essex spinner who suffered the indignity of none for plenty less than a month after taking all ten Littleborough wickets for just four runs (another record). Price remembers Worrell's modesty over his chanceless 152: 'Frankie pointed out that I beat him on at least three occasions and bowled the only two maidens in the 50 overs it took them to score their runs.' Price was relieved before he had the dreaded figures of nought for 100 against his name.

Worrell was renowned for his unselfishness, a quality which was not always to the fore in the Leagues. When Radcliffe came up against Sonny Ramadhin, who later became their professional, Worrell would take his bowling. He played leg-spin well, concentrating, as many West Indians do, on reading the hand. He was not averse, when at the non-striker's end, to shouting 'googly!' to his partner as soon as the ball left Ramadhin's hand. This should not, thought Ramadhin, have been permitted, but it did not impair their close friendship. Against lesser players, Worrell, although competitive, would be considerate. He would keep the ball up to the bat on a rough pitch. 'Ten of those players (the professional was the exception) have to go to work tomorrow,' he would say.

Worrell was to become an excellent judge of any mistakes a colleague was making, indeed a fine judge of a cricketer; but he was not, in his Radcliffe days, considered an effective coach. He was too gentle and probably too shy. His legacy to Lancastrian techniques was transmitted by example.

The hardened League cricketers, men like Greenhalgh, whom Worrell thought good enough to play county cricket, were impressed by his approach to the game; the townspeople appreciated the Worrells' courtesy and standards of behaviour: 'Them's not one thing and say another.' They possessed the qualities northern working people respected: friendliness, decency, directness and openness. A local clergyman, Canon Reg Smith, who played for Radcliffe's 2nd XI, befriended Worrell in a gruff, Lancastrian way. Worrell and Velda, who would sometimes be mistaken for Ramadhin's wife, attended Smith's church as well as the cinema and once, Bolton Wanderers, whose fortunes were to ebb away in tandem with the cotton industry and the Central Lancashire League's gates. Worrell was a good enough footballer to be given a trial by Bury, then in the Second Division, but quickly decided cold weather did not agree with him.

As to the colour of his skin, there were few problems. Once, when bowling at Middleton, scene of his record opening stand, Worrell was abused by a spectator. He glared at the man and proceeded to run through the batting.

In time – he stayed with Radcliffe until the end of the 1953 season – Worrell built lasting friendships. He came to regard the homely suburban town as much his home as anywhere. 'Dear old Radcliffe!' he called it. 'The warmth and friendliness of the people of Lancashire at times left one wondering where the line between one's public duties and private affairs was to be drawn.' He had a rapport with children, whom he coached in the week at school. Joseph Smith, who grew up in the area in the 1950s, would sometimes catch the same train as Worrell on the Bury to Manchester line. Smith said:

> What impressed me most was his essential modesty.
> He was, or seemed, more interested in my school
> scores than in telling me about my heroes. He just
> used to laugh good-naturedly when I asked him about
> himself and turn the conversation back to me.

Smith was sufficiently impressed to write an appreciation in *The Cricketer* and *Wisden Cricket Monthly* on what would have been Worrell's sixtieth birthday.

Yet he remained happiest in the company of West Indians, notably fellow professionals. On Fridays they would flock to his house, initially in Ulundi Street and then in the Bury and Bolton Road, for music, talk and laughter. The Worrells had a friend named Clayton Procope living in Manchester, whose family they had known in Barbados. He, a Trinidadian, shared a flat with two Jamaicans, Ivo de Souza and Herbie Walker, both of whom became High Commissioners. On Sundays they would all meet in Manchester, drink rum-punch or cider and cook the chickens and eggs Worrell was sometimes given in lieu of money for excelling on the field. After lunch they would throw a ball around the sitting-room. Worrell drank heavily in his Radcliffe days – often whisky, brandy or beer – but he endeavoured to ensure it did not affect his game. He did not drink with his Radcliffe team-mates or in public places. He knew that if he failed with the bat the next day, tongues would wag. Even after matches he did not linger, returning to the bosom of his family in the car that Lowe, a generous man, often lent him. Lowe also helped to furnish his house.

At home, Worrell enjoyed cooking. His favourite foods were Indian and Chinese, but he liked the Lancastrian dishes such as hot pot and black pudding as much as the more spicy Bajan fare. Pigs' trotters were a favourite. His brother-in-law, Harold Brewster, a frequent weekend guest whom Worrell would insist on driving back to his Lough-borough home on Monday mornings, remembers him buying a pair of sunglasses to wear when chopping onions.

There was just one blot on those halcyon days. After three years with Radcliffe, Worrell asked his mentor, Lowe, whether there might be an opening for him at Old Trafford. Lowe, as he had done when recruiting Worrell, sought the assistance of the Manchester-based cricket writer, John Kay, who approached Major Rupert Howard, a manager of two MCC tours, who was on Lancashire's committee.

Despite Worrell's growing reputation as a cricketer and a person, Howard was sceptical. He disclosed, confiden-tially, that Lancashire, who had signed the Australian, Ken Grieves, from a Lancashire League club, had given MCC an undertaking that they would take no further advantage of the many international cricketers in the Leagues. There were no immediate registrations for overseas players then but counties could take out special registrations for those who had spent three years in England – such as Worrell. He took the news philosophically. Ironically, Lancashire ultimately did sign a West Indian from the Leagues — Ramadhin — but by then, the mid-1960s, his physique could not take six days cricket a week. Ironically, too, he had been released by Radcliffe.

6

Indian summers and the 'three "W"s'

—— ○○○ ——

Worrell missed West Indies' tour of India in 1948–9 not, as he wrote in *Frank Worrell*, owing to League commitments and a desire to study in England, but because he was not chosen for disciplinary reasons. Against MCC he had turned up late for matches, had upset Gomez, his captain, with his request to go to the airport and he was generally considered to be self-willed and erratic. He asked, as a professional cricketer, to be paid £250 to tour. West Indies Board of Control refused. It was the start of his wrangles with the Board over pay. 'Frank told me later that the shock of being excluded from the touring party was the best thing that could have happened to him,' Gomez said. 'He did all sorts of silly things in those days but he came to value discipline'.

When, the following year, Worrell was invited to join a Commonwealth tour to India, he leapt at the chance. He went on three tours in all, each to India. They were successful both on and off the field. Worrell played what he considered to be the best cricket of his career and his outlook and personality were broadened.

The concept of Commonwealth tours was to bring

together cricketers of more than one country, which at the time was unique. Englishmen, Australians and West Indians from the Leagues were convened in 1949 under the management of George Duckworth, the former Lancashire and England wicket-keeper. Several of the players had not met hitherto and it was thought that the team might dissolve into cliques. These fears were to be proved groundless. Men such as Bill Alley, Cec Pepper, Bertie Oldfield, Leslie Ames, Jim Laker, J.K. Holt jun. and Sonny Ramadhin mixed freely and smilingly accepted the more basic accommodation. The tours were a boon for all India since MCC had declined to send a team there in 1949–50.

Worrell was the star turn. He felt he had a point to make, having been excluded from West Indies' tour. On the first trip he scored 684 runs, considerably more than anyone else. In a representative match at Kanpur he played what in retrospect he felt to be his best-ever innings. He made 223 in six hours 40 minutes on a pitch of coir matting, having to work hard for the runs yet timing the ball perfectly. In nine innings in the representative matches – the series was won by India – Worrell headed the averages at 97.71. He took seven wickets. In all matches he scored 1640 runs and averaged 74.54.

When asked once if he ever drank before an innings, Worrell cited his double hundred in India: 'There was nothing else to do there but drink. I saw so many balls I couldn't miss!' He said to Ramadhin on the voyage out for the third tour: 'You had better prepare yourself now for the drinking you're going to do in India'. There are those who felt Worrell would have been a better batsman, perhaps a more consistent batsman, had he not drunk spirits. Yet his technique was so correct that he still out-stayed others. Certainly the Indians regarded him as the finest batsman of the 'three "W"s' and they had seen Walcott and Weekes in sparkling form the previous year when West Indies toured.

The second Commonwealth tour, in 1950–1, was captained by Leslie Ames, the Kent and England wicket-keeper, with whom Worrell forged a friendship. 'He was one of the nicest men I ever met,' said Ames, 'but he did not take life seriously enough'. Worrell would spend the evenings reminiscing with Ames and others, and the daytime putting the Indians to the sword. He scored more runs than anyone else on the tour, 1900, and was outscored in the representative matches by only one batsman, Jack Ikin, the man who helped bring him to Radcliffe. Worrell also took eighteen wickets in the representative matches, which was more than any other. It all helped the Commonwealth XI to win the five-match series two-nil. Ames suffered from injury during much of the tour and Worrell, at Duckworth's instigation, took over the captaincy on numerous occasions. *Wisden* records: 'Worrell showed himself a capable captain, a responsibility he frequently carried'. Some years later, when Denis Atkinson, a white man who was younger and a cricketer of lesser ability, was appointed ahead of Worrell to captain West Indies, Worrell told friends, 'I had the honour of captaining ten white men in India so that must speak for itself'.

The 1953–4 tour was the least successful, marred by injury and illness. The side was led by Ben Barnett, the former Australian wicket-keeper. Worrell played in just two representative matches, scoring 102 runs at an average of 34, before returning with Sonny Ramadhin to West Indies and another visit by MCC. Only three matches were won by the Commonwealth XI. Yet by then the objective of the trips had been achieved: India's avid public had been stimulated, their cricket improved by the experience. India had the potential, Worrell felt, to be one of the three best cricketing nations in the world by 1967. But, federalist that he was, he was concerned at their provincial outlook, that a potentially good cricketer could be left out of the national side merely because he came from a particular part of the country. Worrell found India, overall, to be a place of 'strange fascination'.

By 1953 the 'three "W"s' were in their prime. Opinion differs to this day as to which was the finest batsman. Between 1949 and 1960 they scored thirty-nine Test hundreds between them and their overall figures are similar. Walcott scored 3798 runs in forty-four Tests, averaging 56.68; Weekes 4455 in forty-eight Tests at 58.61; Worrell 3860 in 51 Tests at 49.48. Yet figures and the fact that each came from Barbados was about all they had in common. Walcott lacked in polish and charm, and at times was reserved to the point of being suspicious; Weekes was small, crude and humorous; Worrell gazelle-like with his nicely barbed Bajan sense of humour. Walcott, who initially played for West Indies as a wicketkeeper, was probably the most difficult of the three to bowl at on a good pitch, particularly in the Caribbean. He could strike the ball with tremendous power off either front or back foot. He was also somewhat self-centred. When, in 1950, West Indies made their memorable total of 730 for three against Cambridge University, Weekes was in line for the fastest century of the season. Worrell continually gave him the strike. Weekes claimed Walcott would not have done that: he would have kept the bowling for himself. Weekes was a compact back foot player, perhaps the most complete batsman of the three. Like Walcott, he pulverised good and bad bowling alike on true pitches and he became, through his Lancashire League experience, as competent on a bad pitch as any West Indian with the possible exception of Headley. Worrell by contrast was full of grace and deft touches, not so sound against pace which perhaps was why he scored fewer runs in the Caribbean than the other two, but the best of the three when the ball wobbled about. Walcott considered Worrell to have more natural ability than he possessed. Worrell, of course, had an advantage over the other two in that he could bowl.

Jeffrey Stollmeyer, who saw the best of each of them, makes this comparison of Weekes and Worrell, whom Weekes considered to be his best friend, in *Everything under the sun*:

> I considered Worrell the sounder in defence, Weekes the greater attacking force; Worrell the more graceful, Weekes the more devastating; Worrell the more effective on soft wickets, Weekes the more so on hard wickets. Worrell gives the bowler less to work on, Weekes has the wider range of strokes. Both are good starters but Weekes is the more businesslike; Worrell appeared to be enjoying an afternoon's sport; whereas Weekes was on the job six hours a day. Due possibly to his wider stroke range, Weekes took more chances than did Worrell and the latter was probably, all told, the sounder in principle but this did not extend outside the realms of actual batsmanship for Worrell was not as capable a runner as Weekes was, nor was he as meticulous over the little accessories that make the complete batsman.
>
> Both men were delightful characters on and off the field, cheerful and humorous. They were both match-winning characters. Worrell, in addition to his batting, bowled left-handed either at a pace well above medium or slow-length stuff. Indeed, he was quite equal to the task of opening our Test attack in 1950, and whenever he bowled his slows he kept the runs down. In the gully or at short leg Worrell took many brilliant catches which, together with his quickness of eye and footwork, were indicative of amazingly quick reflexes. He was the complete cricketer.

Stollmeyer goes on to praise Weekes' slip fielding.

By 1953 Worrell had tightened up his defence as a result of playing on English pitches. He was the most orthodox of the 'three "W"s' despite having been largely self-taught. He would not, for example, attempt to cover-drive an off-spinner who was extracting turn. Generally he would watch the ball on to the face of the bat and play it late, hitting it as swiftly as Walcott without resorting to brute force. When Worrell and Walcott were batting during their record partnership of 574, Worrell reproved his partner for hitting the ball too hard. The fielders, he pointed out, were not having to run.

Worrell's batting average was lower than those of Walcott and Weekes probably for two reasons: they retired at a younger age and they were also probably more concerned than he was with amassing big scores and records. Worrell felt that a batsman should not be judged on the number of centuries he scored. When Worrell went out to bat he was usually in a relaxed frame of mind, often as not having been asleep in the dressing-room. He would wash his eyes out, wander to the crease, greet the wicket-keeper and then enjoy himself.

The 'three "W"s' were friends, certainly; but there were some jealousies beneath the bond. Before and after their playing days Walcott and Worrell did not get on. Worrell had resented Walcott being made vice-captain instead of him for the 1957 tour of England; Walcott in turn seemed to resent Worrell's fame in later life. As batsmen, though, there was markedly little rivalry between the three.

7

North Staffordshire and further education

— ○○○ —

There was, inevitably, competition for Worrell's talents while he was professional at Radcliffe. Two of the leading clubs in the North Staffordshire and District League, Longton and Norton, vied for him: there was some acrimony when Norton won him over, through financial persuasion and the incentive of cricket in a bigger league.

Worrell had a curiously ambivalent attitude towards money. He was generous, as was Constantine, to needy friends in England. He would give away items of kit, particularly when in later years he played for Boys Town. He was generous to teammates. At Norton, collections were taken only for the professional, unlike at Radcliffe, so Worrell chose to share his takings. At the end of the 1950 tour to England, Worrell and Cecil Williams saw the rest of the party off at Victoria Station. Worrell turned to Williams and said: 'You're going to be very lonely. Take my radio – give it back later.' He ploughed personal money into the University of West Indies. He was unselfish to the extent that his wife was unable to keep a rein on his handing out money.

The other persona was the man who had a collection

bag specially made for him at Radcliffe; who refused to tour unless West Indies Board of Control met his financial demands; who, when West Indies captain, instructed the more happy-go-lucky members of his teams that they must not throw away their money gambling. He was always quick to ask for a sum for himself (and for others, too) which was commensurate with his ability. He was, perhaps, the first person to question the fees paid to professional cricketers.

In the 1950s it was common for professionals in the English Leagues to move around if offered more money – their contracts were less binding then than a decade or three later. Worrell, having had five successful – and happy – seasons with Radcliffe, probably needed a fresh challenge. So, at the instigation of Tom Talbot, Norton's chairman and the man who paid virtually all the wages of their professionals, Worrell joined the club in time for the 1956 season, following as professional Alan Walker, the Australian, who had qualified to play for Nottinghamshire. Worrell was doubtless influenced in his decision by the fact that his friend, Manny Martindale, the West Indies fast bowler, had been Norton's professional for three seasons. Worrell's recruitment, needless to say, was heralded as an imaginative move.

Worrell, while continuing to live in Ainsworth, played for Norton on Saturdays for three seasons, interrupted by the 1957 West Indies tour of England. In each year he topped the batting averages for the senior 'A' section. His figures were:

> 1956: 18 innings, 711 runs, average 59.2.
> 1958: 21 innings, 1002 runs, average 77.1.
> 1959: 21 innings, 1014 runs, average 63.4.

Norton finished third behind Longton and Nantwich in 1956, won the championship in 1958 and were joint runners-up behind Ashcombe Park (where Ramadhin was now the professional) in 1959. In 1958 Worrell became the first batsman to score 1000 runs in a season, and also established a batting average record. In the same season he took 67 wickets at an average of 8.4. Norton's new ball attack of Worrell and Ted Smith was generally considered to be the best in their League. Worrell obtained sharp movement off the seam, swung the ball late and at times was genuinely quick off the pitch. Many of the pitches he played on, both for Radcliffe and Norton, suited his quicker style of bowling better. Indeed, he had developed it for that reason. His ability to spin the ball had declined since he cut his left hand at the Empire ground in Barbados.

As at Radcliffe, Worrell was liked and respected. He did not assume that he was guaranteed a place in the team. Having scored a paltry number of runs in his first three matches, he sat in the pavilion and declared: 'I've batted myself into the 2nd XI.' There was, of course, no chance of that happening.

Worrell found the pitches he played on to be drier than those further north and the cricket up to that of the Central Lancashire League. He was, he told the *Staffordshire Sentinel* newspaper, pleasantly surprised by the standard. It was altogether another happy liaison. Anecdotes abound of the man whom the community recall modestly arriving at the New Ford ground by bus, carrying his cricket bag. On one occasion both the captain and vice-captain were away on holiday and Worrell was asked if he would captain the side. He said he would prefer not to do so, preferring to play under any amateur chosen. Then, when he was on the brink of overtaking the league batting aggregate, his chairman wished him good luck. Worrell replied that he was not interested in the record – all he was concerned about was winning the match.

Worrell also acted as deputy professional for Oldham in 1956. In five innings he made only 80 runs but took 17 wickets at a cost of 239 runs.

There was further reasoning behind Worrell's decision to join Norton. The extra money he gained would enable him to turn into practice his strongly held belief that cricketers should educate and improve themselves. He did not see cricket as a life's work. He wanted to ensure he would have something to fall back on after his playing days. Soon after he came to England he had enrolled at the College of Technology (which became attached to Manchester University). There he studied optics for a year but abandoned it through lack of finance and not finding enough time amid tours to fit in all the required reading. Having secured a contract with Norton, Worrell wrote in February 1956 to the Faculty of Economics at Manchester University, putting himself forward as a candidate of mature age. 'If my application is accepted,' he wrote, 'I would like to offer myself for examination in elements of economics, economic history of England and British constitution'. He was accepted as a mature matriculation student and entered the University in October of the same year at the age of 32, reading for a BA in Economics. On his application form in answer to the question: 'What career are you considering?' Worrell wrote: 'A career in industry and trade'. He also stated that he was not liable for national service, was able to attend the university full time and that his interests outside his main academic course were 'all forms of sport'.

Worrell took his studies seriously. He began by reading Economics and French but switched in his second year to a BA Administration, which featured social anthropology. He was supervised by Professor Emrys Peters, who read his essays. Peter recalls:

He was not the most brilliant of students and was a slow worker. He would think getting through two chapters in a week was great. But his English was not bad and he was a thorough reader and a dutiful worker. I thought

he would achieve a comfortable pass. He took an
interest in social anthropology and gained a much better
cross-cultural understanding of attitudes than he would
otherwise have done. I never had to discipline him.

Worrell was one of a handful of West Indian students.
As a Test cricketer he was regarded as a celebrity. He
mixed well: by now he had more white than coloured
friends. 'He was as English as can be,' said Noel Symmonds.
'He always admired the culture, manners and civilisation
of the better type of Englishman'. Students would group
round him in the University bar. But he came and went
quietly, making use of the gym – he was beginning, in his
early thirties, to put on weight – and playing a few games
of cricket for the staff side. He was introduced to it by a
South African professor of liberal leanings with whom he
became friendly, Max Gluckman. Worrell would be first to
arrive, his gear equalling in quantity that of the other ten
players. (He donated a bat to the side.) He would offer to
be placed anywhere in the batting order and would sometimes keep wicket in an effort to stay fit. Before two
pensioners and a dog he would stroke the ball around,
politely thank the captain for the game and disappear
before the drinking started.

It was during his second year that the call came from a
higher level. Worrell, his status now enhanced by attending
a university, was offered the captaincy of West Indies. He
approached Professor Peters for advice, which was readily
forthcoming. 'I advised him to finish his course, thinking
of his future,' said Peters. 'He told me that was his incli-
nation, too. Then Everton Weekes telephoned him, trying
to make him change his mind. I told Frank not to listen'.

It proved salutary, for Worrell gained a BA Admin. in
1959 which led to his post at the University of West Indies.
He gained the captaincy of West Indies, too. No doubt
his degree enhanced his leadership, be it of a cricket team

or a group of students. 'Through studying social anthropology he was able to analyse human beings,' said Cammie Smith, who toured Australia with Worrell in 1960–1. 'He would probe them and could discover why they were not scoring runs.' But whether in 1957 he would have turned the captaincy down had the opposition been England or Australia and not Pakistan, is another matter.

8
Tests and some triumphs
— ○ ○ ○ —

The summer of 1950 belongs to cricketing folklore. West Indies, having been written off after losing the opening Test, won a series in England for the first time, by the margin of three-one in the four match series. Sonny Ramadhin and Alf Valentine became immortalised in the calypso 'Cricket, lovely cricket' which is, today, still sung all round the Caribbean to the bemusement of American tourists.

> With Ramadhin and Valentine
> And give me any nine
> And we can beat England any time

This was given licence: someone had to score the runs. Yet the impact they made was astonishing. They had had barely any first-class experience between them but performed like men with years of cricket behind them. The success of the tour can be gauged by the fact that four West Indians were included in *Wisden*'s five cricketers of the year: Ramadhin, Valentine, Weekes and Worrell.

Worrell, his misdemeanours in the Caribbean behind him, scored 1775 runs in 22 first-class matches at an average of 68.26. He topped the Test averages, scoring

539 runs at 89.83. He also took 39 wickets on the tour. Only Ramadhin and Valentine, who each took over a hundred, returned more. In addition to the brilliance of the 'three "W"s' who scored more than twenty centuries between them, Allan Rae and Jeff Stollmeyer provided solid opening partnerships and John Goddard captained the side fearlessly. Everyone contributed and the party attracted large crowds wherever it went.

The high spot of Worrell's summer was his double hundred in the Trent Bridge Test, one of the innings for which he is best remembered. His score, 261, was the highest made in a Test at Trent Bridge and various other records were set, most notably West Indies making their then biggest Test score – 558 – against England. They were 479 for three at the close on Friday, Worrell and Weekes having put on 241. So well was Worrell playing on an easy pitch that many on the ground considered he stood a good chance of beating Hutton's record score of 364. Yet he was out to Bedser early on Saturday morning, having batted five hours thirty-five minutes and hit thirty-five fours and two sixes. He slept on the floor for some of the match, giving over his hotel bed to his friend, Ivo de Souza, in order to save him money. They played poker on the eve of the Test. Worrell also alternated between bed and floor during the Headingley Test, allowing another friend, Clayton Procope, free accommodation. The manager, Jack Kidney, was not informed and never learnt of it – which was as well for Worrell.

Worrell would assess the state of the game quickly and comment perceptively. He was fifteen years younger than Hines Johnson, the Jamaican fast bowler who celebrated his fortieth birthday on tour, but was confident enough to suggest, during play, where he might bowl. Worrell gave Valentine, like himself a left-arm bowler, every encouragement as he did throughout his career. Likewise did he energise Ramadhin, who had barely been to Port of Spain, let alone out of Trinidad. 'Frankie (Worrell's preference to Frank) practically brought me up,' he said. Even in 1950, a time when it was not contemplated that a black man would lead his country, Johnson marked Worrell down as a possible future captain.

It was a time, too, when Worrell's nurturing on English pitches was paying off. Well accustomed to the wet conditions of an English spring, Worrell, batting first wicket down, played his way into form on all types of surfaces before the first Test. West Indies' strength lay in their batting and Worrell felt it his responsibility to attack the bowling and build on the opening partnerships. This he did to good effect. It was no coincidence that when he failed so did West Indies. In the opening Test at Old Trafford Worrell was dismissed for 15 and 28 – and West Indies lost by 202 runs.

Thus was Worrell a key player for the future. If ever a cricketer can be considered an automatic choice for a tour, then it was Worrell for Australia and New Zealand the following year. He was duly selected but found, after receipt of his contract, that he was being offered more money than some of the other players. He protested to West Indies Board, who narrowed the differential – and regarded him thereafter as a trouble-shooter. The series against Australia, between the two best teams in the world, was an anti-climax. Australia won four of the five Tests and West Indies won only one of their six matches against State opposition. Goddard did not gain the support he received on the tour of England – some of the players were jealous that he was given much of the kudos for that success – and there was further division between Board and players over the itinerary. West Indies were allotted only one first-class match before the first Test. Several players were not at their best, Worrell included. He made one Test century, batting practically one-handed at Melbourne after being hit on the right hand by Keith

Miller, whom Worrell said was the best bowler he ever faced. Worrell's 108 in three and three-quarter hours included only six boundaries. Generally though, he was not at ease against fast bowling and neither were his colleagues. In contrast to Australia, West Indies were handicapped by a distinct shortage of pace so Worrell opened the bowling on several occasions during the series. At Adelaide on a pitch affected by rain that seeped under the covers, he took 6 for 38 and took, in all, 17 wickets in the series.

The party fared better on the New Zealand leg, winning one Test and drawing the other. Worrell made a century at Auckland, driving with a freedom he had not shown in Australia. Those results, though, were not enough to prevent Karl Nunes, president of West Indies Board, stating publicly: 'If we have not the wisdom, temperament or ability to adapt ourselves to the conditions of other countries as we expect them to adapt to ours in West Indies, and if we cannot take what we give, we do not measure up to the calibre of Test cricket.' Nunes' statement was in response to Goddard's comments – to the press – that one first-class match was insufficient preparation for a Test series. The Board suspended him from Test cricket for three and a half years but after that tour West Indies' sides were allotted more matches before the opening Test. 'In the 1950s cricketers did not consider suing for restraint of trade,' said Goddard. 'But if Worrell or Sobers had been suspended there would have been an outcry.'

It had not been a happy tour. Worrell had not enjoyed it, the hospitality apart. He fell out with Goddard, who refused to speak to him the morning after he, Worrell, was out to a poor shot in the first Test which brought Goddard in to have to face the last few minutes of the day's play. Goddard, infuriated, hit a full toss straight back to the bowler. Ordinarily, the two had respect for each other's ability but they were never close. Goddard preferred the company of Walcott and Weekes although he saw little of any of them away from cricket at home. The races went their own way. Miller once attended a party at Goddard's house and asked him why none of the 'three "W"s' was present. 'We do not mix socially,' was the reply, whereupon Miller left and did not return.

For the next three years the captaincy was in the care of Stollmeyer, a wealthy Trinidadian of German and English descent and a top-class cricketer. Even he, a man of forward thinking, had his problems with the Board which culminated in his losing the captaincy to Goddard (whose suspension was by then over) for the 1957 tour of England.

The 1952–3 series against India was won by a Test to nil in spite of discord over selection between island selectors. 'One lesson had been taught me,' wrote Stollmeyer. 'Captaining a West Indies team at home was no bed of roses.' Worrell travelled out to the Caribbean with the Indian team, sailing from Southampton. It was the first time he had been back to Barbados in five years. Having survived a bout of sea-sickness he was accorded an extraordinary welcome at Bridgetown. Some had not forgiven him for leaving Barbados and were upset at his no longer playing for the island, but the majority, unaware he would not be playing for Barbados in the imminent fixture against the tourists, were exultant at his homecoming. The Indians were ignored as Worrell was lifted up and carried shoulder high into Bridgetown from the end of the baggage warehouse.

The mood changed when it was learned Barbados would be without Worrell. Such was the attitude that a Barbados victory over a touring team was welcomed more than a West Indies victory. Barbados did, in fact, almost win. They were defeated only by a tropical downpour.

Worrell played in all five Tests. He scored 237 at Sabina Park in nine and a half hours, and averaged 49 in the series. He took seven wickets at 37 apiece. The matches were memorable for the prodigious batting of Walcott and Weekes, the latter averaging 102 in a high scoring series. Both, in fact, scored more heavily than Worrell against India throughout their careers.

The following year England brought a strong side to the Caribbean under the captaincy of Hutton. It was the first time a professional cricketer had led England overseas. Those who felt that West Indies, too, should be led by a professional (i.e. a black man) now had some ammunition for that thinking although Hutton was not necessarily among them. He went on record as saying that 'the gradual exclusion of white folk is a bad thing for the future of West Indies cricket.'

The series, which ended all-square, was not cordial in relations between the two teams. Hutton told his players to keep their distance, reasoning that too much fraternization would affect their approach on the field. Stollmeyer did not see eye to eye with the president of the Board, Sir Errol dos Santos; bottles were thrown at Georgetown after a run out (as they were on MCC's next tour when a Trinidadian was run out at Port of Spain) and umpiring decisions were contested. All the while there were undercurrents of disaffection among the West Indian crowds. Stollmeyer was jeered at Port of Spain. When he was injured and Worrell, who had been officially appointed his vice-captain, took over, a buzz went round the ground. It dawned that one of the crowd's own was in charge, if only for a short time.

Until the fourth Test at Port of Spain, Worrell had a relatively lean period with the bat. He had been asked to open at Georgetown, which was not his favourite ground, or his favourite crowd. He tended to try too hard when playing there with the result that his natural game did not prosper. He was out without scoring. But in Trinidad all went well, as was so often the case. For the second time, each of the 'three "W"s' scored centuries in the same innings. Weekes and Worrell created a record for any wicket in England–West Indies Tests with a stand of 338. Worrell made 167 and then 56 in the second innings. Although he took only two wickets in the four-Test series, Worrell finished with the highly respectable average of 47.71.

In March 1954 Australia arrived in the Caribbean for their first-ever tour there. Worrell had left Radcliffe and was uncommitted elsewhere. He was therefore available to play for West Indies. Indeed, now twenty-nine, he could reasonably have expected to continue as vice-captain: to the embarrassment of his captain he found himself demoted by the Board and the younger and less experienced Denis Atkinson appointed. Worrell was co-opted on to the selection committee but it was little compensation. Outwardly he hid his disappointment, confident enough even then to express his opinion that he would eventually be made captain, but it could well have affected his game. In the five-Test series which Australia won three-nil, he scored only 206 runs at an average of 25 and took just three wickets. It was the first series he had played in which he had not scored a century, and clearly one he did not wish to remember – it did not receive a mention in *Cricket Punch*. His form was in sharp contrast to that shown by Walcott who hit five centuries and set an aggregate record of 827 runs. One shot illustrated Worrell's summer: in the third Test, when he did play a lengthy innings (56) he changed his mind about late-cutting Richie Benaud and pulled his bat away carelessly, hitting the top of the off-stump.

That summer Worrell took a job at Agualta Vale in the parish of St Mary in Jamaica. He worked for six months on a sugar plantation as a welfare officer-cum-cricket coach for a sports-orientated Englishman, Sir Harold Mitchell. His role was to look after the welfare of the workers and, typically, he ignored the traditional lines of demarcation, treating Jamaicans of bucolic backgrounds as he would sophisticated cricketers, without taking sides.

West Indies' next scheduled tour was to New Zealand in 1955–6. Stollmeyer declined to go and the Board decided to send a party of young players under Atkinson. Worrell, too, opted not to tour, remaining in England to make preparations for further education and the continuance of his career in the Leagues. Walcott also chose to stay in West Indies so the batting was carried by Weekes and Goddard, who went as player-manager. The series was won by three Tests to one but the younger players, whose number included a promising cricketer by the name of Garfield Sobers, achieved little.

Stollmeyer's last remaining ambition was to lead his country on their 1957 tour of England. But by then he was considered injury-prone and Goddard, overweight but as combative as before, resumed the leadership. From the outset, though, the team split into factions, which developed on the voyage to England. On that voyage Walcott, by now captain of British Guiana, was appointed vice-captain, to Worrell's displeasure. The Board made the error of appointing two managers, Tom Peirce and Cecil de Caires, with the result that members of the party played one off against the other. The tour, said Worrell, was destined to fail.

Worrell, even though he was not always in agreement with Goddard, never gave less than his best. Goddard admitted that had he had the co-operation from others that he received from Worrell, the outcome might have been different. Walcott did not pull his weight as vice-captain and both he and Weekes, past their meridian, struggled with the bat. No one looked after the young players and Ramadhin, whose bowling represented West Indies' best hopes of success, was collared in the first Test by Peter May and Colin Cowdrey in their remarkable fourth-wicket stand of 411. West Indies rarely got away to a good start with the bat and lost three of the five Tests.

Worrell had a successful but disjointed tour. He topped the batting averages, scoring 1470 runs at an average of 58.80, but compiled only 350 runs in the Tests, and one innings accounted for 191. He headed the Test bowling averages, opening both bowling and batting in the fourth and fifth Tests. This was after going in seventh in the first Test, sixth in the second and opening in the third. His innings of 191, unbeaten and his fourth highest Test score, was at Trent Bridge where he was on the field throughout play from 11.30 on Thursday morning to 3 o'clock on Monday – a total of twenty and a half hours on the field. *Wisden* states that 'It is probably the longest time any cricketer has endured'. Worrell carried his bat that innings, scoring 26 boundaries in just over nine and a half hours after opening the bowling in England's first innings. Of his innings he wrote:

> People compared it with any big innings they could call to mind which just proves how valueless to cricket statistics are. It was far from being my best-ever innings . . . the bowler gets no assistance at all at Trent Bridge and any batsman who has a sound defence and one – yes just one – scoring shot will be able to score a century.

When West Indies followed on, Goddard sent Worrell out again to open with Sobers in murky light. Godfrey Evans, England's wicket-keeper, was startled to see him. As Worrell passed, Evans enquired why he was batting again. The reply was typically laconic: 'I've come out here to develop a few photographs'. He held out for an hour before Brian Statham bowled him with one that moved in late. That evening Worrell was unable to walk from his room to the dining-room of the Station Hotel in Nottingham. His feet were bloody and blistered to the extent that Vic Lewis, the band leader and cricket enthusiast, had to prise his socks off with hot water. There was scant time for rest as Worrell was combining cricket with academic work during the tour. Yet he managed to enjoy himself. On the Saturday night of that Test, when the press were under the impression he had gone home to study, he embarked on a three-hour drinking spree at 3 a.m. with fellow students and players.

Worrell had met Lewis during his Radcliffe days when he went to see Lewis and his band at Blackpool tower. It fuelled Worrell's interest in jazz and subsequently he played for Lewis' 'showbiz' XI whenever he could. It was Lewis who helped to quash Worrell's plans to take a West Indian side to South Africa in 1959 at the invitation of non-white South Africans. Worrell had readily accepted, feeling it would help to break down apartheid: he had been promised matches would be arranged against multi-racial teams. He organised a scratch side, had ties made in the same colours as Lewis had for his XI – mauve, green and blue – and ordered long and short sleeve sweaters. There were protests, inevitably, from West Indian politicians. Some English politicians also questioned the sense of the tour. In the West Indian press Constantine debated the rights and wrongs with C.L.R. James, the writer and Marxist philosopher, who supported Worrell. Ratial Patel, President of India's Board, urged that the tour be called off.

The strictures of Lewis, who had been in South Africa with his band, made more of an impression. 'I think when Frank had heard several stories of mine, he was persuaded not to go. The country was in a mess when I was there and it would have been impossible then for his team to stay in a first-class hotel,' said Lewis. Worrell never went to South Africa, during or after his playing days.

Later that year Worrell returned to the Caribbean for the 1959–60 MCC tour, having obtained his degree. Gerry Alexander, the wicketkeeper, was West Indies' captain, his accession detailed in another chapter. Worrell, the people's choice for the captaincy, helped their cause in the four Tests he played in – an ankle injury kept him out of the third Test – making 320 runs at an average of 64, a considerable improvement on earlier series in the Caribbean. West Indies still lost, by a Test to nil, but Worrell gained a satisfaction from the tour more meaningful than the transience of victory and defeat. He was booed when he went out to bat at Bridgetown in the first Test but showed again how good his temperament was for cricket at the highest level. With Sobers he put on 399 in nine and a half hours, the best fourth wicket stand by any country against England and the highest for any wicket against England. His innings stretched either side of the rest day, Sunday. Making a big score on his home ground was ideal: he drank through to dawn on Sunday morning, spent the day in a haze and had another beano on the Sunday night. When he resumed his innings on Monday morning, he was in a stupor. That, and the application which went into his century exhausted him at a time when his captain wanted the scoring rate stepped up. He managed only 20 runs in two hours ten minutes in spite of professing 'to wanting to sun them some more'. E.W. Swanton wrote in the *Daily Telegraph*: 'Worrell's failure to respond to the needs of the situation and indeed to the command of his captain from the pavilion balcony was the more disappointing because it was so unexpected.' Alexander declared with Worrell three short of a double hundred (17 fours, two sixes in 11 hours 20 minutes) and there was no dissent. Yet Worrell had scored his first Test century at Kensington Oval: for the first time in a long while he had some empathy with his own kin.

9
Captaincy

— ○ ○ ○ —

Contrary to some belief, Worrell was twice offered the
captaincy of West Indies before he accepted it: for the
series at home against Pakistan in 1957–8 and then against
India and Pakistan in their countries in 1958–9. As ever,
Worrell put his studies first. Cricket he saw as a means to
enjoyment, not his life's work.

Worrell was under some pressure to take the captaincy,
and not merely from the likes of Everton Weekes. The
colonial period was nearing its close in the Caribbean.
Two of the foremost islands, Jamaica and Trinidad, were
seeking independence. Black men were moving into pos-
itions of power in government and commerce. The hopes
and expectations of the West Indian populace, their history barely forged, lay with the one non-white cricketer
who, it was felt, could realistically become captain. Worrell
had proven himself leading the Commonwealth XI. He
was by now a cricketer of wide experience who knew the
game as well as anybody, he was more mature, and he was
undertaking a degree course which was testimony to his
intellect (and few West Indian cricketers were graduates).

The captaincy, the domain of whites, had long been a

tangled issue, owing, in part, to the very geography of West Indies. Each island is a separate territory with separate government and separate culture. Worrell's first Test series illustrated the insularity prevalent at the time: a Jamaican chosen as captain for the Test in Jamaica, a Trinidadian in Trinidad, a Bajan for the other two. That same tour, it was held that Jamaica would not have played MCC if Headley had not been appointed captain. Two years later there was a groundswell of opinion that he should lead the 1950 tour to England. Undoubtedly he should have captained West Indies in more than just one Test. He played, though, in an era when it would not have been thought dignified by some whites to have a black man leading West Indies on to the field at Lord's.

There had been white men who excelled as leaders: H.B.G. Austin, a son of the Bishop of West Indies, succeeded in allying some method to much natural ability early in the twentieth century; Jack Grant, a Cambridge Blue, led West Indies to their first victory abroad, in Australia in 1930–1. Gomez, Stollmeyer and Goddard were liked and respected, Goddard, although his knowledge of the game was limited, for his leadership on the 1950 tour of England. It was in the mid-1950s that the inevitable process by which captaincy ceased to be the preservation of the white man was stymied. In 1953–4 Worrell was chosen to be Stollmeyer's vice-captain for England's visit. Yet before West Indies' next series, against Australia, Denis Atkinson, an allrounder who rarely led Barbados, replaced Worrell as Stollmeyer's deputy. It was, according to the fair-minded Stollmeyer, a preposterous decision and one which was the cause of much dissension and bad cricket played by West Indies during that series. Atkinson, in fact, was pitched into the first Test as captain owing to Stollmeyer's injury. Several players who were senior to him did not give him their full backing. At the same time, West Indies Board decided to revert to a selection committee of four men, one

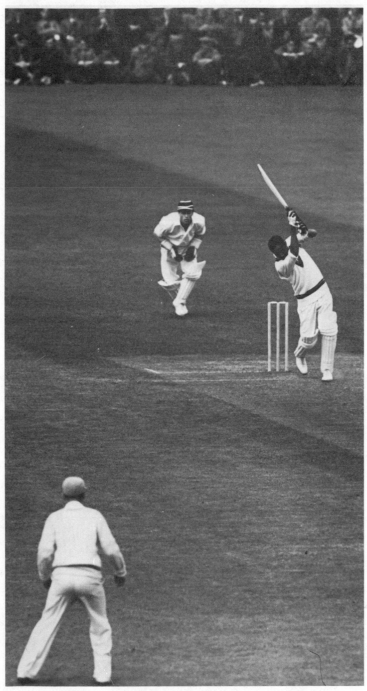

4 West Indies v Cambridge University at Fenners, May 1950. Worrell plays a powerful off-drive. (Photo: BBC Hulton Picture Library)

5 The 'three "W"s' share a joke at a reception in London in 1957. From left, Frank Worrell, Everton Weekes, Clyde Walcott. (Photo: The Press Association Ltd)

6 Colleagues and friends, Worrell (left) and Weekes walk out to resume their partnership at Fenner's. They put on 350 for the West Indies against Cambridge in May 1950, which was a record. (Photo: BBC Hulton Picture Library)

from each of the major islands, and the captain. Stollmeyer, in his autobiography *Everything Under the Sun*, wrote: 'The system merely encouraged infighting and parochialism.' It was not until two decades later that Stollmeyer, by then on the Board, gained sufficient support for a selection committee of three, drawn from any of the islands, plus the captain, which helped to overcome the last vestiges of insular thinking. It was no coincidence that West Indies' domination of Test cricket then became absolute.

Soon after Atkinson was made vice-captain, he was also named to lead West Indies' tour of New Zealand which was not to take place for another year. His vice-captain was appointed as well. Bruce Pairaudeau was another white man. The timing was in itself extraordinary, but more significantly the selections lacked in credibility. Neither man was experienced in captaincy or a cricketer of the stature of the 'three "W"s' who were in their prime.

Clyde Walcott wrote later in his book *Island Cricketers*:

West Indies had no delusions, nor false politeness, about the strength of New Zealand cricket, and they had decided to send a young side, omitting all but a few of our established Test players. The choice of Atkinson as captain – to gain experience – as vice-captain against Australia was in line with this policy. The public were not slow to ask why the 'three "W"s' had been left out of the reckoning, particularly after Frank Worrell had been vice-captain against MCC during the 1953–4 series. The public feeling seemed to be that the West Indies Board did not relish the prospect of having a coloured captain, but I do not think this was, in fact, the case. Much more likely, it seemed to me, was that West Indies were following the old-fashioned precedent of standing out against the professional captain: a precedent which, despite Len Hutton's reign as captain, still had its roots deeply laid in England.

Nevertheless, the gamble of bringing Goddard out of virtual retirement to lead the 1957 tour to England had not paid off. Goddard by then was past his best and the party was split by factions. Then when Worrell declined the captaincy, the Board turned to Gerry Alexander, a light-skinned Jamaican and a Cambridge Blue who was a Test-class wicketkeeper batsman in his own right. The home series against Pakistan was comfortably won, Walcott and Weekes representing their country for the last time (Walcott was to come out of retirement against England in 1959–60). They had struggled in England but played on, not wanting it to be thought that they were retiring through being passed over for the captaincy.

Alexander was re-appointed to captain in India and Pakistan in 1958–9. The first leg of the tour resulted in victory for West Indies but was marred by strained relations between Alexander and Roy Gilchrist, the volatile fast bowler: Gilchrist was sent home for bowling beamers in the nets before the party moved to Pakistan. This series was lost. By the time they returned to Trinidad and the tour by MCC, Worrell was back from England. Alexander, feeling that Worrell had been the captain-elect after the 1957 tour, assumed Worrell would now be appointed. Yet, as a result of the success in India and also, Alexander felt, as an endorsement of his disciplining of Gilchrist, the Board persuaded him to continue. They felt he was more familiar with the abilities of what was now a young team than Worrell, who was out of touch with West Indies cricket.

It was not a decision which pleased the populace. They aligned themselves with Gilchrist – because he was one of them more than for anything else – and with Worrell, who, they felt, could handle him. They knew that Worrell, whom they wanted as captain, was worshipped by Gilchrist. Worrell was his surrogate father: Gilchrist would consult

him on everything, down to buying a shirt. Worrell felt
Gilchrist could be handled effectively – he said so on the
BBC World Service, expressing the opinion that Gilchrist
should be 'helped' back. There was a feeling also that
Alexander might be too close to MCC's captain, Peter
May, having played at Cambridge with him.

Disaffection, though, was constricted in the Caribbean.
The protestors needed a mouthpiece. C.L.R. James had
returned to Trinidad, island of his birth, to edit the political paper *The Nation*. When the MCC tour drew near, he
announced his intention through his medium to propose
that Worrell be appointed captain. Indeed, it was not so
much a proposal as an all-out campaign. 'My argument,'
he said, 'was simply this: there was not the slightest
shadow of justification for Alexander to be captain of a
side in which Frank Worrell was playing.'

James, who felt the Board should listen to Worrell and
accept an apology which Gilchrist would be helped to
write, launched his invective before the end of the second
Test in Port of Spain. By that stage the crowd were in a
state of fermentation, agitated by stifling heat, gambling,
West Indies' poor cricket and tight umpiring decisions.
One of these resulted in the local boy, Singh, who was
playing in his first Test, being run out. James thought they
were agitated most of all by years of discrimination. When
Singh was run out the bottles flew, and flew so fast that the
match was interrupted before England won it.

Worrell himself was not in complete agreement with
James' conduct, even though in *The Nation* mention of
race was avoided. His reaction to being overlooked was
never verbose: it amounted to no more than a sad shake of
the head. In *Frank Worrell* Ernest Eytle does not touch on
the subject or on the riot: the Test merits a skimpy para-
graph. Alexander, who kept wicket brilliantly during the
series, also detached himself from the polemicists, not

reading the papers or giving interviews as is the modern way. But members of Alexander's team were unsettled and protested to James, who none the less did not relent.

'E.W. Swanton said that Worrell would have been appointed in any case,' said James. 'We, who had seen our black people neglected for 25 years, could not think that way. To ask us in our struggle to accept that was asking too much. I don't believe the cause suffered from our anger.'

In retrospect, James wrote in his book *Beyond a Boundary* that his advocacy was unfair on Alexander. 'I put my scruples aside and I think that for the first, and I hope the last, time in reporting cricket I was not fair.' Some critics deplored it, former players thought it over-emotional and even dishonest since Worrell had twice turned down the captaincy. Atkinson was informed Worrell was not interested in taking it on. Be that as it may, James' writing had a startling effect on a Trinidad public whose appreciation of Worrell had been axiomatic since his first tours. James wrote:

> Australia wants Worrell as captain. As a man he made a tremendous impression in Australia. Thousands will come out on every ground to see an old friend leading the West Indies. In fact, I am able to say that if Worrell were captain and Constantine or George Headley manager or co-manager, the coming tour would be one of the greatest ever.

James made it clear that if the rejection of Worrell continued he would – reluctantly – raise the racial issue.

Ultimately it was not just pressure from journalists or the West Indian public which persuaded the selectors to appoint Worrell – it was pressure from Alexander. The series against England had been lost, West Indies having been beaten in that ill-fated Port of Spain Test. Alexander, by now suffering from 'Worrellitis' as he put it, was available for selection as captain to go to Australia on the next scheduled tour. But he was equally content to play under Worrell, whom he liked and respected. He was aware of the difficulties inherent in captaining and keeping wicket. West Indies Board met to debate the captaincy at their headquarters in British Guiana under the chairmanship of John Dare for two full days. They appointed Gerry Gomez manager, Max Marshall assistant manager, and Frank Worrell captain. Gerry Alexander was made vice-captain. There was no dissension from Board or public. All classes approved. The tour that did more for cricket than any other had taken shape.

10
The father figure

—— ○ ○ ○ ——

The game is greater than the result, or so it seemed at the end of West Indies' 1960–1 tour of Australia. The two countries added a new dimension to Test cricket in a series of unparalleled excitement. There was sportsmanship and no little ability, too. The game was recharged, both in Australia and elsewhere. It was almost forgotten that West Indies had lost the series, albeit by the narrowest of margins. In his first tilt at the captaincy Worrell exploded the old myth that someone from his background, i.e. a coloured man, could not captain West Indies successfully. He did so with a different style of leadership from what had hitherto been known in a colonial environment, which was 'do so because I say so'. Worrell charmed, encouraged, led and corrected. The casual spectator who did not know the players would be unaware of who the captain was. Fielders moved into position as if programed. He needed luck, as any captain does: he had in his tour party the most talented generation of cricketers to emerge in the Caribbean. Worrell's task was to give them direction and his success in so doing is how he is best remembered. Had he failed, and we can see from history that the West Indies Board never tolerated failure for long, cricket in that hemisphere would not have developed to the supremacy of the last decade. That is not to say the Board would necessarily have reverted to white captains, for by then there were not many left; but failure – failure to make an impression – would, felt Worrell's opposing captain, Richie Benaud, have set their cricket back twenty years. Instead, Worrell led West Indies into the comity of nations.

Some of his predecessors, such as Denis Atkinson and Gerry Alexander, felt Worrell stood little chance of failing. They knew he would make a good captain, being tactically sound if not innovative. They knew he would be respected and that he had fine players. The choice of Gomez was for once an inspired selection by the Board. Worrell had long respected rather than resented him for the disciplinary action Gomez took when Worrell flouted the rules in his first Test series. 'Gerry,' Worrell would say in Australia, 'that was the best thing that ever happened to me'. He talked much to Gomez of his youth, the way his life had been shaped, and his belief in predestination. This extended to cricket. 'We'll make 250 runs today,' he would say, and be only ten runs out.

From the outset when the party arrived in dribs and drabs, Worrell complaining of food poisoning, he and Gomez decided to concentrate on good public relations. They stressed, as Benaud did, that entertaining cricket was the aim and they proved it could be embraced with the prime objective, namely to win. Worrell and Gomez resolved to answer all questions the Press put to them and subsequently gained their support. One journalist even apologized and withdrew criticism of Worrell's decision to play Rohan Kanhai in a match when it was discovered Kanhai had left the field suffering not from a recurrence of the old injury but from a nosebleed.

Yet the tour began badly. Having beaten a Western Australian Country XI by an innings, West Indies lost their first State match, to Western Australia, by 94 runs. Their batting was indifferent and undisciplined and Bobby Simpson, Western Australia's opening batsman, scored 308 runs against them. In their next match, against an Australian XI, West Indies dropped numerous catches which led to victory slipping away. They drew again against South Australia, unable to score 181 at 84 an hour. They did, however, defeat Victoria by an innings and 171 runs, the State collapsing against Ramadhin and Valentine after Kanhai had made a double century, but the pen-ultimate match before the first Test resulted in an innings defeat by the strong New South Wales side. Worrell, who had shown good form in the first matches, constantly making middling scores, alone batted well in the first innings, scoring 51. He pulled a leg muscle and did not bat in the second innings when West Indies were bowled out by Benaud. Worrell missed the drawn match with Queens-land in which rain washed out play on the last day.

After the defeat in their first State match, West Indies had their first of only three lengthy team talks on the tour. The selection committee decided to keep all the players informed of their decisions: in the past this had by no means been the case. It was also planned that at team meetings any player would be allowed to speak his mind. Throughout the tour Worrell paid particular attention to the younger players. He arranged the seating on the flights, sitting each one next to an experienced member of the party. He encouraged discussion, often in hotel rooms at night where he could escape the hangers-on. He was compassionate to those who were out of form, inviting a given player to dinner with him. He would not accept social invitations unless the other players were asked as well. From these informal talks he analysed a player's strengths and weaknesses, assessing his temperament and ability against different types of bowling. He would casually introduce a subject into conversation, which was not

7 Early season practice on West Indies tour of England, 1963. The non-striker is Deryck Murray, West Indies wicket-keeper. (Photo: The Press Association Ltd)

8   With the British Prime Minister Harold Macmillan (now Lord Stockton) and Ted Dexter, captain of England, at Chequers in 1963. In the background is Iain Macleod. (Photo: Times Newspapers Ltd)

9   The Mansion House, London, 1963. Worrell and Velda exchange a gift with the Lord Mayor of London, Sir Ralph Perring, and his wife at a function to conclude West Indies' tour of England. Sir Ralph said, 'A gale of change has blown through the hallowed halls of cricket.' (Photo: The Press Association Ltd)

restricted to cricket. Barbados, where a greater sense of equality was by now prevailing, was a favourite topic: Worrell seemed intent on correcting the view that some Bajans still held of him.

Worrell would tolerate dissension with his arguments but not dissension – or swearing – on the field. Against the Australian XI Sobers was adjudged lbw, a decision which he clearly disputed. Worrell, at the non-striker's end, glared at him, made a few comments and during the next interval told all his players that there was to be no questioning of umpires' rulings. Thereafter West Indies players walked both when given out lbw and when they knew they had hit the ball if caught. The Australians respected them for it and Worrell enjoyed a rapport with the umpires.

Worrell looked upon the State matches as preparation for the Tests. He was not too concerned if West Indies did not win them. As a result, perhaps, of Goddard's criticism of the itinerary for their previous tour of Australia, there was plenty of preparation. West Indies played New South Wales a second time and were again beaten by an innings. Worrell's side were aghast that, on winning the toss, he gave New South Wales first innings on a brown pitch likely to take spin. Worrell's reasoning was that he wanted to expose his batsmen to playing on such a pitch to attune them to those conditions at Test level.

The series is remembered as much for the tied Test as anything else. This was at Brisbane in the very first encounter. It was, moreover, the first time a Test had finished in this way. It has been described as the greatest cricket match, even the greatest game ever played with a ball. The cricket was compelling and of the highest standard long before the extraordinary final over in which three wickets fell.

From the start West Indies attacked, Sobers scoring a magnificent century in just over two hours and Worrell, who went in at five, making 65. Alexander hit a half-century, as he did in every Test in the series. Australia responded with a first innings of 505, Norman O'Neill making 181, which gave them a lead of 52. West Indies' batting in their second innings was less convincing, only Worrell – who again scored 65 with some high-class strokes – and Kanhai batting well. Australia thus needed 233 but time was at a premium. They lost five wickets for 57, four to Hall and one to Worrell, and their sixth fell at 92. Then the drama began.

Davidson, who had a splendid all-round match, was joined by his captain, Benaud. They put on 134 and were still in partnership half an hour before the end, with only 27 needed. Worrell then gave Hall the new ball. Davidson and Benaud had run some cheeky singles but, having whittled the target down to seven, went for one too many: Joe Solomon pounced on the ball at mid-wicket and threw down the stumps with Davidson a yard from the crease.

Wally Grout, Australia's wicket-keeper, took a single off the last ball of Sobers' over, which meant six runs were needed off the final eight-ball over, to be bowled by Hall. The first ball hit Grout high on the leg and he and Benaud scampered a single. Benaud, on 52, went to hook Hall's next ball, a bouncer, got only a touch and was caught behind: Australia were 228 for eight. Worrell had expressly told Hall not to bowl a bouncer, which he reiterated when Hall went up to him with a big grin. 'But I got him out,' said Hall. 'That's not the point,' said Worrell.

The new batsman, Ian Meckiff, pushed the third ball of the over back to Hall. Five balls left, five runs to win. A bye came off the fourth ball and the fifth was skied by Grout to the leg-side. Hall, following through, lost his nerve and the catch. A single resulted. The next ball was clouted by Meckiff to leg. He and Grout ran two and turned for the winning run. Conrad Hunte picked up the ball on the square-leg boundary and threw it to the wicketkeeper – hard, low and true. Grout flung himself at the crease, sliding in on his forearms but could not beat the return.

In came the last man, Lindsay Kline, to face the final two balls with the scores level. He placed the first one from the unflagging Hall to square-leg and went for the run. Meckiff backed up well but with little more than one stump to aim at, Solomon again threw the wicket down.

Worrell was, he said, the only player on the field aware that the match had been tied. He said he had not been nervous, merely concerned that his players might have lost their nerve. They would, he felt, have done that in the past, so in the closing stages he went round the field calming them down. When the crowd jeered Hall for bowling a bouncer, Worrell told him to bowl another. It was, no doubt, one way of ridding Hall of tension.

Benaud told Worrell it was the greatest game he had played in – few could have thought otherwise – and that it was the way cricket should be played. The sadness was that only 4000 spectators were present at the end of the match. Even commentators and writers had departed, convinced that Australia were going to win comfortably.

Being the first Test, it set up the series. There was no shortage of spectators attending the second encounter at Melbourne: a crowd of 65,000 watched the third day's play. Australia, having won the toss, scored 348, 'Slasher' Mackay 74 of them. West Indies, having been 124 for two, were dismissed for 181 and made to follow-on. They fared little better in their second innings despite a century by Hunte, their total amounting to 233. Worrell bagged a pair. Australia, needing only 67 to win, scored the runs for the loss of three wickets with a day to spare. After the euphoria of the first Test, it was a dreadful anti-climax for West Indies. There was despondency rather than recrimination. Valentine, upset for Worrell as much as for himself, burst into tears.

West Indies picked themselves up with victories over a Combined XI and Tasmania before the third Test at

Sydney. For this, they brought in Lance Gibbs for his Test debut, leaving out Ramadhin who had taken wickets in the State matches but had made a lesser impact in the first two Tests. It was a difficult decision but Worrell got it right. Gibbs took eight wickets in the match, helping West Indies to a 222-run victory. Sobers, too, was in tremendous form, making 168 out of West Indies' first innings' score of 339, in which Worrell scored 22. The pitch took spin and Valentine and Gibbs made use of it, Valentine capturing four wickets in Australia's first innings of 202. West Indies began their second innings badly but Worrell and Cammie Smith regained the initiative with a fourth wicket partnership of 101 in 67 minutes, Worrell making 82 not out. One of his strokes had the crowd on their feet. He stood up to his full height of five foot ten inches and elegantly drove Davidson to the cover boundary. Gomez turned to his players and said, 'You've seen it all now, you can go home'.

Alexander chose an opportune time to score his first Test century and Australia were left with the nigh-impossible task of making 464 on a turning pitch. Neil Harvey and O'Neill batted soundly but Gibbs countered their hopes on the fifth morning. Australia's last eight wickets fell for 59.

The fourth Test, played at Adelaide after two victories by West Indies over Country XIs, ended in almost as exciting a finish as the tied Test. Kanhai made a century in each of West Indies' innings, adding 107 with Worrell in the first innings in just over an hour. Worrell made 71 and 53 and Alexander again scored heavily, to the delight and surprise of his teammates. Australia in their first innings almost matched West Indies despite Gibbs taking a hat trick but, set to score 460 in just over six and a half hours, lost their first three wickets for 31. Despite a determined stand between O'Neill and Peter Burge, they collapsed to 207 for nine. When Kline joined Mackay an hour and 50 minutes remained. Two minutes later Sobers, almost on top of the bat, claimed a catch off Worrell's bowling. It was turned down and the pair, incredibly, managed to play out time and add 66 runs.

So the series, level at one win apiece, could not have been better stage-managed. The teams met at Melbourne again for the final Test. West Indies were put in by Benaud, the atmosphere heavy. They made 292, Sobers the top scorer with 64. Worrell batted at number five as he did for most of the series and was given a resounding round of applause out to the wicket. Alas, he did not progress beyond double figures. Australia retorted with 356 before a world record crowd of 90,800. At the end of the third day, West Indies were 62 runs on with eight wickets left but the balance tilted Australia's way when play resumed on the Monday. Alexander maintained his record of having exceeded 50 in each of the Tests but he received scant support from the remainder of the middle order. Worrell was out for 7 and his side for 321, which meant that Australia required 258 for victory. Simpson again got them away to a good start and despite a minor collapse, Worrell taking three wickets, Australia got home with two wickets in hand.

The tour was wound up with a match against the Prime Minister's XI at Canberra. It was here that Worrell had one of his occasional disagreements with Sobers. As Sobers was the key player in the side, Worrell wanted him to play before the prime minister. Sobers refused, feeling he deserved a rest. Rather than make an issue of it, Worrell let him have his way.

No one had been more taken with Worrell than Sir Robert Menzies who, as the fixture would suggest, had a passion for cricket. He would arrange his trips to England to fit in with Test matches. He particularly admired Worrell's approach to the game and his rare combination of personal distinction and readiness to talk to anybody.

At the end of the tour Menzies said to him: 'The next time I meet you I hope it will be as Sir Frank.' The recommendation to the Queen for a knighthood would in normal circumstances have come from the Prime Minister of Barbados – but as Sir Grantley Adams did not attend the Commonwealth Prime Ministers conference in March 1961, Menzies most probably had more than a say in mooting it.

Worrell had made an impression which had permeated Australia, where many people were unaccustomed to black people. West Indies had held the interest of Australians throughout, indicative in the crowd figures, the large profit made on the tour and the institution of the Frank Worrell trophy, to be contested by Australia and West Indies in future series. The players, some of them for the first time, had enjoyed participating in Test cricket. They had not objected to a tightening of discipline: Worrell had asked his players to be in their rooms at 10 p.m. during matches and there had been no leeway for senior players. But at the end of a Test, the champagne would flow. More than once Worrell had lost his voice owing to the strain of captaincy but he would recover it around 1 a.m. through imbibing. Sometimes it was particularly clear that that moment had arrived: Worrell would start to sing his favourite hymns after a few drinks.

Worrell was fair to all his players. His friendly relationship with Benaud and their approach to the game rubbed off on the teams. Consequently such controversial umpiring decisions as there were the players took in the spirit of the game. On the eve of West Indies' departure from Australia, a little footnote was put in the *Melbourne Evening Herald*, stating that West Indies would be driving round Melbourne on their way to a civic reception from the Mayor of Melbourne and their departure. Most people in the city could have known of this only when that edition was printed, yet half a million people saw them off, throwing ticker-tape at their open top cars and pleading 'Come back soon'. It was a farewell that has never been accorded a cricket team before or since. Tears welled up in Worrell's eyes. He knew he would never return to Australia as a cricketer.

On return from Australia Worrell considered retiring. The tour had taken much out of him, physically as well as emotionally. Although by then he had shed the nervousness which had often made him feel sleepy throughout a day's cricket, he would return to the pavilion and slump into a corner after a day in the field. He stayed close to the wicket not merely for the purposes of captaincy but to give himself less ground to cover. He would bowl himself in short spells.

Worrell was approached to become a Hall Warden at the University of West Indies shortly after arriving back in Jamaica and took the post up. Had he not been allowed leave to play cricket it is likely his career at Test level would not have continued. His appointment at the University took effect in September 1961; five months later he was leading West Indies again, this time against India.

India had never won a series against West Indies – nor even a Test – but they had good reason to hope for better things to come. They had beaten England in 1961–2. As it was, they left the Caribbean thrashed by five Tests to nil and their captain seriously injured. Nari Contractor, who was also an opening batsman, was struck on the head in the match against Barbados halfway through the tour. It was a misjudgement on his part – the ball did not get up above stump height – but the incident was much publicised owing to Contractor's skull being fractured and because the young fast bowler, Charlie Griffith, was no-balled later in the match for throwing. Contractor was rushed to hospital for an emergency brain operation which saved his life. Three of his team gave blood for him, as did Worrell, who provided more than anybody.

Hall had told the Indians at the start of the tour, 'Wait until you see this fellow Griffith – he's quicker than me.' Griffith himself maintains he never bowled faster than in that match – he felt he had to prove himself to get on the tour to England the following year, and the Indian players were undoubtedly frightened. Although he took wickets in that match, which Barbados won by an innings, Griffith was not picked for any of the remaining three Tests. He felt the press were against him and that he was being saved for the tour to England.

Yet the tour was more than a year away. In fact Worrell refused to have him in his team, also being of the opinion that Griffith threw. Later, Worrell would defend him against such allegations, not because he disagreed with them but because he thought Benaud, a prime critic of Griffith, was hypocritical. Australia at the time had bowlers whose actions were under similar suspicion. Griffith did tour England in 1963, successfully in spite of being under the scrutiny of the press. At the start of the tour the journalist Crawford White asked Griffith to demonstrate his action in his overcoat on Paddington Station for the benefit of a photographer. Worrell refused to allow it.

India were stunned by Contractor's injury and were never in a position to challenge West Indies' dominance. They won only one first-class match on tour. For Worrell the series was as much a triumph with the bat as with the captaincy. He topped West Indies' batting with an average of 88 and a highest score of 98 not out. The pace of Hall, the spin of Gibbs and the all-round abilities of Sobers were the other telling factors.

West Indies' tour party of 1963 was arguably the strongest they have taken to England. Worrell thought it to be the best balanced he had played in, on and off the field. Most of the batsmen had Test experience; several had played in the Lancashire Leagues. Gibbs had emerged as an off-spinner of excellence; Hall, Griffith and Lester King were genuinely quick; Sobers had developed his faster style of bowling to the point that he was hostile. He had a splendid tour emerging, as Everton Weekes prophesised, as the outstanding cricketer in the world. Yet it was only thanks to Worrell that he went at all, having been offered less money to tour than he would have received playing League cricket. West Indies were again most popular tourists, the crowds thronging the grounds to see them. They won the series by three Tests to one, and left England feeling they had elevated the status of the West Indian in England.

Worrell was now 38 and carrying some excess weight. Before the tour he cut out alcohol, ate less and had numerous sessions in the nets at Sabina Park. He had said he would tour, assuming he was selected, only if he felt fit enough. He had shown in the series against India that there was little wrong with his form, but then form is a two-edged sword. It was clear that in 1963 he was past his best as a cricketer. He made some contributions, batting at seven and even eight in the Tests and having useful spells as a change bowler. An English journalist could still write of him: 'An innings by Worrell knows no dawn. It starts at high noon.' Irrespective of the outcome of the tour, he decided beforehand to retire at its end.

Worrell's ambition for the tour was to establish West Indies as an international side which would be asked to make frequent returns. He did just that. It had been six years since West Indies last came to England; their next scheduled tour was brought forward to 1966, so popular was Worrell's party. In his summary of the tour, John Arlott declared that through the joyous West Indian supporters, 'we heard the history of English cricket change.'

The tour began rather more promisingly than had the 1960–1 visit to Australia. Four of the first five matches were won. In the first of these, against Colonel Stevens's XI at Eastbourne, Worrell made 73 in West Indies' first innings total of 188. It was self-evident that his players had lost no respect for him. They regarded his praise as an honour in itself. Some of them asked Alex Bannister, the cricket writer, where the nearest betting shop was. 'You won't tell Worrell, will you?' they said. Mindful of his own extravagance with money in his younger days, Worrell had banned gambling among his players during matches. He also stopped them from playing cards in the evenings. He reasoned that it strained the eye, which could not adjust from the number on the card to focusing on a cricket ball. Only Sobers dared to disobey Worrell – and was left in no doubt that it would not be advisable for him to gamble again.

As in Australia, Worrell paid especial attention to the younger players. He persuaded Dr Eric Williams, Prime Minister of Trinidad, to finance Deryck Murray's university education. Murray, on his first tour, was from Trinidad and academically inclined. Worrell told Basil Butcher, in two words, to slim. Butcher was running round the ground early the following morning.

Tactically aware though he was, Worrell had less of a grasp of the rules and regulations governing cricket matches. In the traditional opening first-class match of the tour at Worcester, Worcestershire set West Indies 162 to win. They fell well short, in spite of having seven wickets intact. Worrell was under the impression there was no tea interval on the last day and had paced the innings accordingly.

In their next match West Indies beat Gloucestershire by 65 runs, Griffith taking eight for 23 in Gloucestershire's innings of 60. Worrell had swiftly analysed Griffith and discovered the knack of being able to make him bowl to the very limit of his ability. Worrell would walk up to him and say, smiling elegantly, that he was the only man who could change the course of the game. 'I'm not telling you to bowl, I'm asking you. If you're tired you can go and see the "physio" afterwards.'

The match against Gloucestershire is also remembered for Sir Learie Constantine's intervention in a concurrent dispute at the Bristol bus company, who had refused to employ coloured crew members. Leaflets protesting at the ban were handed to West Indies' players when they arrived in Bristol. Some were clearly upset but Worrell refused to get caught up in it. 'We do not want to be involved in political matters,' he said. Constantine's respect for him did not diminish because of it – on the contrary, he made a speech to the Royal Commonwealth Society in which he praised Worrell's leadership and spoke out against those who had held him back. 'People less talented than Worrell, less knowledgeable, have been selected as captain before because we had a South African attitude in West Indies,' he said. In the Caribbean, if not in Bristol, things were changing. Under-privileged coloured cricketers, Worrell felt, were now more than mere performers and were no longer denied full expression.

In their remaining matches before the first Test, West Indies continued to sweep most opposition before them. They beat MCC, Oxford University, Somerset and Glamorgan, and were beaten only by Yorkshire, for whom Freddie Trueman took ten wickets and scored 75 runs, being once out. Yorkshire were the only side other than England to beat West Indies in first-class matches but West Indies were to gain their revenge in the return encounter.

The opening Test at Old Trafford attracted 67,000 people over four days. Four days, because West Indies had no need of the fifth. They beat England by ten wickets on the Monday afternoon, having outplayed them at every facet of the game. *Wisden* takes issue with West Indies only over their returns to the wicket. Upon winning the toss – Worrell maintained it gave a side a 20 per cent better chance of victory – Hunte made 182, then Kanhai 90 and

Worrell an unbeaten 74, his highest score of the series, as it transpired. It contained just 29 scoring shots, 15 of them boundaries and was made out of 103 in 95 minutes. West Indies declared at 501 for six and, on a pitch receptive to spin, Gibbs bowled out England twice, taking five for 59 and six for 98. It was West Indies' sixth successive Test victory – a record.

The series, though, was set up by the second Test at Lord's. Just as the tied Test in Brisbane had fired the public's imagination for the remainder of the series so now this match did the same. Even when only one over remained, there could have been any one of four results – a victory for either side, a tie or a draw. It was, in fact, drawn, England being six runs short of their target and West Indies needing one further wicket. West Indies had again won the toss and led England, for whom Ted Dexter played one of his finest innings, scoring 70, by four runs on first innings. In West Indies' second innings, Butcher and Worrell put on 110 for the sixth wicket, Worrell making 33 and Butcher, who was ninth out, scoring 133. England needed 234 to win.

At tea on the last day they were 171 for five, which was effectively six as Colin Cowdrey had had his left arm broken by Hall. Fred Titmus and Trueman then went to successive balls, and Brian Close, his policy of moving down the wicket to Hall and Griffith having worked for a while, was out for a courageous 70. Worrell said that he felt Close's train of thought to be wrong. Derek Shackleton, who had been recalled for this Test, joined David Allen with 19 minutes remaining and 15 runs required. They whittled it down to eight needed off the last over, bowled by Hall. Two runs came from the first two balls but Shackleton was run out off the fourth – by Worrell, who by this stage was as nervous as anybody. But he kept his composure, picking up the ball from short-leg and, rather than shying at the stumps, beat a fellow thirty-eight year-old for speed to the other end. Thus Cowdrey had to come in again with his arm in plaster, two balls left and six wanted. Worrell went up to Hall and said, 'Remember, Wes, if you bowl a no-ball you won't be able to go back to Barbados'. This so terrified Hall that he ensured he bowled from behind the crease. He kept up his pace until the end, stung by Worrell's retort when he pleaded fatigue. 'Who's the fastest bowler in the world, Wes?' Worrell asked him. 'Me,' said Hall. Worrell replied: 'You the fastest bowler in the world and you can't keep going?' Hall charged in but not at Cowdrey, who did not have to face a ball. Allen played the last two defensively.

Around 125,000 people had watched the five days, and immediately advance bookings for the third Test at Edgbaston were boosted. This match was won by England by 217 runs, Trueman taking 12 for 119, the best Test analysis of his career. There were few big scores. Worrell himself made 1 and 0, and although the pitch was fast and true, his team was dismissed for 91 in their second innings, having been set 309 to win.

The sun came out for the fourth Test at Headingley; West Indies seemed to play better when it did. The match was almost an exact reversal of the previous Test, West Indies triumphing by 221 runs. Sobers made a century and Kanhai 92 in West Indies' first innings 397. Griffith took six for 36 in England's 174 and, after Butcher had made 78 out of 229, England were unequal to the task of scoring 453 to win.

In the final Test at the Oval, West Indies underlined their superiority. Sobers and Kanhai were injured but opted to play – Worrell said this would not have happened in the past – and West Indies won by eight wickets with a day to spare. The gates were closed on the fourth day with more West Indians in the crowd than Englishmen. Griffith again took six wickets in an innings – and was warned for short-pitched bowling – but West Indies none the less trailed by

29 runs on first innings. For the last time that he would walk to the wicket in a Test match, Worrell was given a standing ovation. He made 9 before Statham bowled him.

However, West Indies then bowled out England for 223 and scored the 255 they needed for victory for the loss of only two wickets, Hunte completing another hundred. West Indies' supporters poured over the outfield and clamoured for their heroes. Worrell, though, was lost in thought, paying no attention to the cheerful noises around him.

Worrell was honoured with the freedom of the city of Kingston on his return to West Indies; the Barbados government gave him a State reception; Norton awarded him a benefit match; Radcliffe named a street after him and the Queen knighted him at Buckingham Palace after an announcement in the 1974 New Year's Honours List. Worrell gave a lunch party on New Year's Day and, typically, mentioned nothing of it.

11
Mortar and gown

— ooo —

The University College of West Indies was founded in
Jamaica in 1948 as a residential seat of learning for men and
women with the target of growing from an initial intake of
33 students to around 750 in ten years. Thus accommodation was planned on the campus, at Mona, just outside
Kingston, for Halls of Residence. Each of these was to be
headed by a Warden who would be a full-time member of
the academic staff, living in a house within the hall complex. His job would be to oversee the running of the hall
and its facilities, including dining-room and kitchen, and
to provide leadership and guidance to the students. This
was styled on the roles of heads of colleges at Oxford and
Cambridge. The first of the permanent halls was completed in 1950 for 160 students, initially women. It was
named Irvine Hall after the committee on the Asquith
Commission, set up to look into higher education in the
colonies. Its first warden was Philip Sherlock (later Sir
Philip), who was Vice-Principal of the College.

By October 1959 the number of students had grown to
695 of whom 249 were women. One block in Irvine was
kept reserved for them. The following year Vice-Principal

Sherlock left to head the University College's expansion at St Augustine, Trinidad, and afterwards another block was added for 120 students at Irvine, who would be entitled to reside in Hall for only their first two years. The time was right, it was felt, to recruit a full-time Warden for Irvine.

The students were pressing for more assistance with sporting activities. There was no director of sports at Mona (indeed, one was not appointed until 1965). It was felt that the warden of Irvine should be a person who could assist in the promotion of sport. Worrell, obviously, was in the limelight following the 1960–1 tour of Australia. Many members of the staff as well as students had spent sleepless nights listening to the broadcasts. Sir Sidney Martin, who became registrar and then a Pro Vice-Chancellor, went to bed reconciled to defeat in the tied Test. He was awoken at 3 a.m. by roars from students which indicated that West Indies were still battling. It was also, of course, known that Worrell had procured a degree. He was approached on return from the tour by the Vice-Chancellor, Sir Arthur Lewis, and appointed warden of Irvine in April 1961. He took up his duties that September.

Thus Worrell had the full support of both students and staff. He was elected in the first instance for three years; in due course the post became an appointment of a limitless tenure.

It was a time of change. Staff and students alike were enthusiastic over the formation of the Federation of West Indies. Plans were well advanced to petition the Queen for a Royal Charter establishing the University of West Indies (as it now was) as a full degree-granting institution. It was all new ground for Worrell. He, Velda and Lana soon settled in to the three-bedroomed warden's house but approached campus affairs with circumspection. Worrell was diffident, somewhat shy even, and it took him a while to gain confidence. He was helped by informal conversations with fellow wardens and discussions with the Vice-

Chancellor. In a BBC interview with Rex Alston in 1963, Worrell described his role as 'pleasantly harrowing.' He was, he said, 'in loco parentis to students, an administrator responsible for moral welfare and discipline, a personal adviser. I drift in the breeze.' He also did a little tutoring. He had an unwritten agreement that he could obtain leave to play cricket. Various people stood in for him including Professor Eric Ellington, who became a close friend.

Worrell was soon involved in the planning of sports and recreation. He helped draw up plans for the extension of the students union and the design of a new pavilion as part of the improvement to the playing fields. Both were complete by 1965. He organised soft-shoe football and re-designed the cricket field, transporting clay for the pitches in his Jaguar. The four halls, which were formed in a cluster to the south-east of the main campus, were within walking distance of the lecture rooms, the University hospital and the students union, but the playing fields, to which was added an Olympic-size swimming pool, were further distant. The men's halls in particular kept pressing for more sporting and recreational facilities within the compound and the wardens were perturbed at the proliferation of cricket being played with a tennis ball on the pathways between the blocks. There was also concern at increasing rivalry in some inter-hall games, particularly football games, which were turning into skirmishes. As a result, the University's teams suffered. Worrell conveyed that concern in an article he wrote for the student quarterly magazine *Pelican*, entitled 'Gentlemen, the University.'

It is a source of great disappointment to me personally to find that in a male student population of over 600 there is comparatively little interest in health preserving games. When one compares the performances of the players from clubs where the number of playing members is in the region of 30 with the performances of the young and virile of this

University, one sees how far short the students fall of the requirements. What are the factors responsible for this state of affairs? Are the students less capable as footballers, cricketers, etc than the players off campus?

I will state most catagorically that we have potentially more international material on campus than any two clubs outside. Where are we failing?

I think that the University sportsman needs a new orientation. He displays a lack of purpose and devotion to his sports. Many of the undergraduate sportsmen are lazy; others are yet to be convinced that a mean can be struck between their mental and physical exertions. I cannot see that anything which is likely to make the individual healthier can fail to make him better; others are so orientated towards that bit of paper that they spend their three or more years convincing themselves that they cannot find the time from reading to spend six hours a week on the playing fields.

People of every country have come to expect leadership in every field from university graduates. The universities of England, India and Pakistan have provided the cricketing leaders of their respective countries. The students of this university who left their secondary school as accredited sportsmen must be made to realise that they owe it to their country and to this university to find the time to contribute something to university sport. There are far too many youngsters around us who are thinking only of receiving and not giving. Their government gives them scholarships which they accept as a right, the lecturers impart the desired knowledge which they regard as an obligation, services are provided in the Halls of Residence which they consider they are entitled to. The scholarship, tuition and service they get will in due course enable them to earn a living for their families. Have they ever stopped to ask themselves what they have given in return? I doubt it.

I would like to suggest to you all that a way of training yourselves in the desirable attitude of giving is for those of you who have the ability (and there are many) to use sport as a first avenue.

Year after year we hear the records of Chancellor Hall from Chancellorites. I must confess that having been associated with cricketers for the past 26 years in which environment the only taboo is on self-praise I find the bragging of these young men particularly galling.

Not once have I heard anyone attempt to compare the standard of the football of any one year with that of a previous year so as to find out whether the standard is improving or not. This seemed unimportant to the student. The youngster's only interest is in sticking their chest out and without any suggestion of conscience they cannot forbear to tell everyone how good they are.

This greatness apparently stems from playing one match and winning one. I hope and pray that one day someone will wake up and ask for a comparison of this hall standard with that of the city teams.

Another disturbing feature of the undergrads' attitude to sport is revealed in their replies to questions on their absence from the playing fields. Some argue justifiably that late lectures are mainly responsible, but for every such reply one hears four others say that it is too far to travel to the playing fields. I wonder how many players throughout the world do have a shorter distance to travel from their offices or homes to their clubs.

No one on campus will deny that there is much more sporting talent in Chancellor Hall than in the other halls but it is unfortunate that their goals are so low – to regard the winning of a match against any hall as the epitome of any sport is a waste of time and talent. In the future let us think of the University: let us not indulge in the twentieth century's most deplorable reject – the malpractice of telling other people how good we are. Do let us give the other halls and guests an opportunity of congratulating us on our performances. Let us continue to keep both feet on the ground. Let us not fool ourselves that manifestations of egotism are construed by any but those involved as contributing to hall spirit.

We have got to stress the necessity for frequent practice and humility if we are to realise the ambition of seeing this University supply the clubs, the islands and the West Indies with the creative leadership that is so sadly lacking today.

Gentlemen, the University!

Worrell would toast his hall only after he had toasted the University at Irvine dinners. He wrote:

It is annoying to find a campus of men without the ability to see the wood from the trees. For two years I have witnessed the undergraduate body go wild over a hall match and at the same time display no interest in the University's football. I am at a loss to find out what purpose this hall football serves. I would have thought that if we were at all concerned about the public image of the University these hall matches would have been kept in their right places, i.e. as a step towards University representation.

The University teams were often slack and lackadaisical before Worrell arrived. Jamaica's Board of Control threatened to throw the University out of the Senior Cup competition: Worrell used his influence as a member of the Board to retain their status. (After Worrell left Mona, they did not remain in any competition.) In the hope of encouraging higher levels of performance and interest, a system for the award of University colours in various sports was introduced in 1964 at the instigation of Worrell and Sherlock. Worrell himself participated in some weekend games since members of staff were permitted to play. David Holford, who attended the University before playing for West Indies, recollects Worrell fielding at leg-slip in an inter-campus cricket match and picking up the ball with his back to the batsman while pretending to run after it. The unsuspecting batsman set off for a single whereupon Worrell turned and threw his wicket down.

Worrell would give subtle advice to the captain, Michael Clarke, which reflected his sensitivity. Once, he arranged a match at his old firm, Reynolds. On this occasion Clarke, who kept wicket, was among the opposition. Worrell duly reached a half-century and then told Clarke to stump him. Worrell made the dismissal appear unscripted, which only a fine batsman can do, and hence offended no one. Clarke kept the story to himself until Worrell died.

In an attempt to further standards on the campus, Worrell pumped some of his own money into the re-designing of the cricket field. He gave out of his pocket to other causes, too. He spent 700 Jamaican dollars (£200) on having Irvine Hall ties made (he was never fully re-imbursed). He liked and often wore striped club ties himself and was concerned about the standard of dress in Irvine. It smartened up considerably during his years as Warden. (Worrell had become noted for his appearance, on and off the cricket field. He would rub the ball in the lining of his pocket rather than redden his flannels and it was rumoured that he would buy a pair of shoes rather than polish old ones.)

In 1964, Worrell's last year at Irvine, he visited Barbados, Trinidad and British Guiana to encourage businessmen and others to contribute to an appeal launched by Princess Alice, the University's chancellor, in view of the forth-coming grant of full status and an expansion in student numbers. Later that year Worrell undertook a similar mission in Britain. He was present when the chancellor inspected the temporary site of the University buildings at the campus in Barbados on 13 March while she was on a tour of the eastern islands in the Caribbean. When sufficient funds had been raised through the appeal for the development of playing fields and the construction of a sports pavilion from an area comprising a crop of cane, Worrell was invited back to Barbados to give advice. He went there regularly in 1966 and finally early in 1967 when the ground was levelled and planning for a cricket pitch could commence. He had discussions with the Building Advisory Committee and the University's architects, and immediately spotted that the straight road planned from the foremost access road to the front entrance of the main building would limit the distance of the boundary.

Worrell told the assembled company that they should remember the Sydney Cricket Ground had a 90-yard boundary and that the students should be accustomed to such a distance in case they were ever picked for a tour to Australia. It was a measure of the breadth of his thinking. He pleaded for a curve to be put in the road which would lengthen the boundary. By that time plans had been drawn up for a hall to be sited on the other side of the road with one block to be built just where Worrell wanted the curve. Just in time, the Canadian architects were asked to move the hall's buildings back by ten yards. Worrell got his longer boundary, even if it did not stretch to 90 yards.

Worrell had asked for the sports pavilion to incorporate two changing-rooms, for home and visiting sides. Funds for it had been donated by Barclays International and Messrs Stewart, Smith and Co. on the understanding the pavilion was named 'The Barclays-Stewart Smith pavilion'. When the tenders came in prices had risen and it seemed one changing-room would have to be omitted. Worrell said that if this were done the other one might never be built. He strongly recommended a further approach to the firms, who increased their donation. Two changing-rooms were built. Sadly, Worrell did not live to see them.

In 1963, the year after Worrell went to Irvine, Jamaica was granted independence. One of the vehicles of government in Kingston was the Legislative Council, which after independence became known as the Senate. Modelled on Britain's House of Lords (although membership was not hereditary) membership, which was unpaid, carried prestige. It incorporated a cross-section of the community: those nominated had to be of some standing and integrity. The Senate did not carry quite the power of the House of Lords – it could delay government decisions but not overturn them. Few initiatives were taken and it met only on Fridays. It was, though, effectual for the opposition in that their views could be aired in the chamber and, more significantly, in the press. Worrell joined as a nominee of the government, his name put forward by the Prime Minister, Sir Alexander Bustamante. Another member of the Council was Michael Manley, who later became Prime Minister. He and Worrell were among eighteen men and three ministers who formed the Senate, presided over by a President, clad in a gown. The members wore suits.

Worrell never had strong political views. It was expected he would follow Bustamante's Jamaica Labour Party line – which, contrary to what it might suggest, was mildly conservative. Worrell's outlook was, in terms of Caribbean politics, middle-of-the-road, or in the British sense, old-fashioned liberalism. He joined on 8 May 1962, taking his oath and seat on 30 November. That same day he made the first of only two speeches in two years. The debate concerned the Jamaica Government Securities Bill. Worrell's feeling was that Jamaica should preserve the marketability of existing Jamaican Government stocks in the United Kingdom. The text of his speech was:

> Mr President, I support this Bill. For a long time Jamaica has been raising money in the UK market and in the foreseeable future it seems that we shall continue to do

so; and it is very important that we try to preserve our status and also the status that exists on the stock market; also to take steps in order to issue any future government stocks in the English market.

As regards the issuing of future Jamaica stocks, I gather that negotiations are currently going on and we hope that this would lead very shortly to suitable arrangements. This Bill which is being introduced is a means towards putting ourselves on an even keel in this sort of venture; and it gives me great pleasure to support this Bill, the purpose of which is to confirm the undertaking given on the 31st day of July 1962, by the Government of Jamaica in regard to Jamaica Government securities (*cheers*).

The Bill was passed.

Worrell's second speech was just fourteen days later, this being on the Rent Restriction Port Maria, Oracabessa and Highgate Orders 1962. It read:

I do not think I am wrong in thinking it is the desire of every man and woman in the society to realise an improvement in the standard of living. And it is the Government's duty and determination and (I go as far as to couple the Opposition in this) it is everybody's duty and determination to assist the people in this area.

Now one of the greatest sociological hindrances to the achievement of this aim has been the high cost of rent charged throughout the country. I am told that as much as 40 per cent of the breadwinner's income has got to be allocated to rent. And when compared with possibly 15 or 20 per cent in other civilised countries in the world, one can see the crippling effect this has on the hopes and aspirations of the people.

In order for a family to realise its rent and to discharge its financial obligations, the husband alone cannot manage and the wife has to go out to work. This has a very serious effect on the family because more often than not this wife has got to commit the kids more or less to the guidance and surveillance of domestic help, with the resultant hue and cry of deterioration in the standard of discipline (*applause*).

If we can get these rents reduced, it will do a lot of good towards relieving the frustration that lots of the breadwinners of the country seem to experience. When we deduct, for instance, these rents from the normal wages of the worker, what is left really is a mockery when there is much to be met. So that the Government's decision is to try and remove some of the abuses which need adjustment and find an equitable solution to this very difficult problem.

I feel sure that the Opposition will go along with us in this hope, and I have very much pleasure in seconding this Resolution (*applause*).

This, too, was passed.

From 15 December 1962 to 24 April 1964 when he resigned before his departure for Trinidad, Worrell chose not to participate in the affairs of the nation, although he attended the Senate regularly. He was accepted and liked by the other members and felt honoured by his nomination but it was thought he did not enjoy the life of a Senator. Worrell had no intention of extending his career in politics beyond the Senate. 'I do not fancy the mud-slinging of electioneering. There are no written rules in that,' he said. He was not an effective debater, being too dignified and diplomatic, qualities better suited to speaking at cricket receptions. Even then Worrell was grateful for help. In his time as West Indies captain, Conrad Hunte, a man of strong convictions, would often advise him on what to say in his speeches. Regular speaking at cricket dinners requires a fund of stories and jokes. This was not Worrell's forte.

Worrell's second sojourn in Jamaica was notable in other ways. Having played for Kensington, it was expected that he would either rejoin them or go to one of the other well-known clubs: several clamoured for his expertise. Yet he chose instead to play in the slums of West Kingston with underprivileged boys for a club named Boys Town. It had been founded in 1940 with the motto 'We build.' Its objectives, symbolised in its crest, appealed to Worrell. It depicted mental, physical and spiritual ideals: a boy reading a book, two boys playing cricket and in the centre, the cross. Under the directorship of the founder, the Revd Dr Hugh Sherlock, brother of Sir Philip, it aimed to provide basic education, training for employment, mental, physical and spiritual growth and 'the opportunity to become good and useful citizens.' Boys came to play at Sabina Park rather than watch from the trees. The reggae singer, Bob Marley, grew up in Boys Town, and indeed became a good and useful citizen.

In 1960 the troubles that befell the Jamaican economy, the mass unemployment, political strife, vandalism and deterioration in moral standards were but in their infancy. It was just a year since the club's most famous sporting son, Collie Smith, had been killed in a car crash in England when on the verge of great things as a West Indies all-rounder; he had been guided by Sherlock and to an extent by Worrell. Worrell had helped overcome his major weakness as a batsman which was to play the ball that left him. The road in which the club is situated in Kingston 14, is named after Smith.

Worrell played, unpaid, on Saturdays for Boys Town for two seasons. They took part in the Senior Cup Championship, which is under the umbrella of Jamaica's Board of Control, one game lasting two Saturdays. Rather than lead the side, Worrell said he would prefer to play under the incumbent captain, Cleveland Richards. It would, said Worrell, help him to get to know the boys. Richards demurred, saying Worrell was too great a cricketer not to captain, so Worrell was appointed and immediately led Boys Town to success. They won the 1960 Senior Cup for the first time, defeating Worrell's old club, Kensington, at Boys Town Oval. It gave the youngsters the confidence they needed. Worrell himself batted high in the order but did not make many runs, an exception being when the Cup was won. This match, in fact, was played over three days. Kensington batted through the first Saturday and part of the second, setting Boys Town 168 to win. When Worrell came in, Lester King, then a raw fast bowler – he played for West Indies the following year – was on. His first ball to Worrell, who effectively stood between Kensington and victory, struck him on the pad, plumb in front. Everybody appealed but the Test umpire, Douglas Sang Hue, did not move. There was utter silence around the ground. Worrell went on to make 70, not being dismissed until victory was assured.

It did not especially matter that Worrell did not score prolifically – his contributions of leadership and inspiration were of greater value. He also helped to raise funds for development. 'With quiet dignity he made the poorest boys feel important,' said Sherlock. 'He put more in than he took out and his values, standards, integrity and fair play showed religious convictions.' Boys Town, funded by the Government, Kingston firms and the public, built on the success Worrell had helped achieve, survived the traumas of the 1970s and continued to flourish in the 1980s.

12
The last years

— ○ ○ ○ —

Worrell, happily ensconced in the university, might well have stayed in Jamaica had it not been for the entreaties of Velda. She had become a part-time social worker but her close friend, Dolly Springer, wife of the registrar, had left the campus and most of her friends remained in Barbados, the other end of the Caribbean. She devoted herself to the well-being of her husband, but his peripatetic life never suited her.

So in 1964 Worrell decided to take up a job offer in Trinidad, the island being less than an hour's flight from Barbados. Worrell was appointed by Dr Eric Williams, Prime Minister of Trinidad and Tobago, to be consultant on community development, working in collaboration with 'The Better Village Programme' which was initiated to improve living standards in rural districts. For a year Worrell organised cultural activities, for which his studies in social anthropology stood him in good stead. He was aided by Gary Sobers, who was not, for once, suffused in cricket. The two of them organised coaching, with the assistance of Rohan Kanhai.

By now, all doors were open to Worrell. He would never

again have to walk Bridgetown's Broad Street in search of employment. He chose to stay in Trinidad and remain an academic. 'He demonstrated his love of the university and its students, refusing other job offers and insisting on working for the university,' said Sir Philip Sherlock. The university's third campus is sited on 500 acres near the foothills of the Northern Range. Away from the bustle of Trinidad's capital, Port of Spain, expanses of lawn are dotted with laboratories, offices, lecture rooms, halls, and a variety of trees and shrubs which evoke its history. St Augustine, as it is called, pre-dates Mona. It was for forty years the home of the Imperial College of Tropical Agriculture, specialising in research and training for agri-culturalists throughout the Empire. In 1960 this became the Faculty of Agriculture of the University of West Indies.

The original hall, taken over with the other Imperial College buildings in 1960, was Milner Hall. This was remodelled and took in 108 students. Another hall was built in 1963 with funds from a Canadian firm. It accom-modated 192 male students. This was officially opened in January 1964 and named Canada Hall. By October 1963 there were 583 students including evening students, and only 300 places in the two halls. One block in Milner was for women. The number of full-time students who had to live out was proportionately higher than at Mona, so it was decided to establish a post of dean of students (as had been done at Mona in 1962) who would also be warden of both the halls. His especial responsibility would be for living-out students.

Worrell was appointed as dean of students (a promotion from being a warden) and warden of these two halls. In a report for 1964–5 it was stated that 'the appointment of a dean has helped immeasurably in liaison.' In the cricket reports for the same academic year is written: 'At the start of the season we were indeed fortunate to have with us Sir Frank Worrell, who kindly agreed to play in our senior grade team, and much of our early success must be attributed to the solid support he gave in all departments of the game.' Reference is also made in that report to Worrell being among the half-century makers and as one of those who had 'excelled on occasion with bat and ball.' There is a reference to a forthcoming inter-campus tour in Mona – the first of its kind.

That same university year the 'Friends of the University' was established in Trinidad and Tobago to raise funds for the St Augustine campus. Through that group's activities funds were raised *inter alia* for the development of better playing fields and for a sports pavilion, in the planning of which Worrell played a leading role. Each morning he tended the cricket pitch. The fields were named after him. Fund-raising continued after his death, but although an issue of stamps depicting Worrell brought in several thousand Trinidad dollars, runaway inflation meant that the pavilion was not built. The university is still hoping to procure funds from Trinidad's government.

As Warden, Worrell went about his duties much as he had done in Jamaica – quietly and effectively. A Sub-Warden of that time, Baldwin Mootoo, remembers that he had 'enormous moral authority'. He would see students in the study of the detached warden's house, built in 1946 of wood and a corrugated iron roof. As at Mona, he had free board and lodging and a university gardener tended his garden. But there was no cook or maid provided.

Worrell enforced the strong line on discipline he took at Mona. In an address to students at a sports colours and awards ceremony in June 1966, Worrell advised them to put much into what they hoped to get much out of. Referring, no doubt, to his early days in Barbados, Worrell recalled that there was a time when leadership came from a certain sort of man – 'and this was based on nothing more than he was a certain sort of man' – but the present tendency was a striving for merit. And the individual who had the scope could still obtain his or her degree as well as make headway in sport. He hoped the time would not come when the people of the Caribbean would find a situation in which the holders of first-class honours degrees from the University of West Indies would be denied opportunities in preference to those with pass degrees from universities abroad.

Worrell did not believe that expending energy on the playing fields affected the quality of degree obtained. He cited the examples of David Holford and Deryck Murray, both Test cricketers, in support of his argument, and added that the individual who could bring a fit body to his work would, obviously, assimilate more energy than the individual who stuck only to his books. He said he did not know if a society was needed with 'all brain and no brawn' but one 'of hypochondriacs' was not required.

Worrell then referred to 'the lack of a responsible approach' to sporting activities at the university two or three years previously and warned that if its reputation in sport was tarnished 'it will follow as day the night that the reputation of the university will be tarnished in work situations.' Before congratulating the recipients of awards, Worrell suggested that if they found themselves in outlying villages or districts they should pass on some of their knowledge of particular games to the younger ones. 'You have attended this University and come out with a degree, and I think they will regard you as a sort of authority and this will assist you in arrogating yourself to such a description.'

By the mid-1960s Worrell was reasonably well off. He bought a house in the parish of St Thomas in Barbados named 'Welches'. It was known as 'the great house of the plantation'. He intended retiring there or conceivably living in it while working at the campus in Barbados. Neither was to be; Velda thought it to be too big for upkeep and Worrell sold it shortly before he died.

Worrell was able to give Lana a public school education in England at Wycombe Abbey following her early schooling at Whitefield preparatory school near Manchester and at St Andrew's Girls School in Kingston. Even so, the hefty fees were, inevitably, a strain on his salary and emoluments from *Cricket Punch* and *Frank Worrell*. It was the practice of black people of wealth or status to send their children abroad to be educated and Worrell was a West Indian who was shaped by western civilisation. The sophistication and good manners he possessed and so admired were Bajan qualities – had he been living in Barbados he might well have educated Lana there – but Bajan qualities acquired from Britain. 'Although our basic education in West Indies is good,' Worrell said, 'social graces are not as much in evidence as in England.' He took a deep interest in Lana's schooling, helping her with her French which he spoke fairly well. And he taught her to drive in his Jaguar when she was twelve, the two of them circling the playing fields of Mona. The lessons continued in Trinidad. It was Worrell's intention to send his daughter on to finishing school in Switzerland but after his death finances dictated that she went instead to the Lucy Clayton Secretarial School in Kensington, London – which was no less prestigious. She was contented both there and at Wycombe Abbey.

Generosity was one of Worrell's finest traits. He would give items of his cricket kit to students and poor children in Boys Town, seeking no publicity for so doing. He gave readily of his own money to the university, individuals and causes, which did not always find favour with Velda. Between 1962 and 1964 he supplied two teams in the Jamaica Netball Association with gear and uniform and paid their affiliation and league fees. They were named 'Maglinnes' after his middle name. One of these became the leading team in the 1962–3 season, sweeping all opposition before them. It supplied three players to the

10   With Sir Learie (later Lord) Constantine, March 1963. (Photo: BBC Hulton Picture Library)

11   As Dean at St Augustine, University of West Indies: speaking at the second annual sports colours and inter-clubs committee presentation of awards at the Student Union in June 1966.

12 Worrell shortly before his death in 1967.

Jamaica side which toured England in 1963. Worrell found time to visit them during the West Indies tour.

Worrell continued to travel, both around the Caribbean and to England. He raised funds for the university, saw old friends and played some cricket. At a meeting of the International Cricket Conference, he proposed that bowlers' run-ups be limited to twenty-two yards. (This, of course, was before any restriction was dreamed up for limited-overs cricket.) In 1964 he commented on the England-Australia series, sitting in the press box alongside Keith Miller and C.L.R. James. In one way he preferred life there: like many a cricketer before and after him, Worrell was not altogether enamoured with the press. In 1959 he wrote: 'Sad to say, sensation appears to take precedence over news, especially in England where the standard of cricket writing has been gradually on the decline. More and more inaccuracies seem to appear year by year'. Of the Australian press, he told Reuters in a 1965 interview: 'The Australians are the nicest and friendliest people . . . . However, over the past two years some of their sportsmen-turned-writers have done a great deal of harm to the reputation of their country and its wonderful people.' No doubt Worrell was happiest sticking to the rudiments of the game in his own articles, notably for *The Observer*.

In that summer of 1964 Worrell played in a number of friendly matches. He represented Free Foresters, one of the best-known of club sides, against Oxford University; MCC; Lord's Taverners; led a West Indian XI on three occasions (which developed into the Rothman's World Series); played in a testimonial match for Terry Spencer, the Leicestershire bowler, at Loughborough, and in a benefit match for Henry Horton, the Hampshire batsman, at Lord Porchester's ground near Newbury. These were his last games in England.

Later that year and early the next, 1965, the first series between West Indies and Australia for the Frank Worrell trophy took place, in the Caribbean. Sobers, Worrell's protégé, was appointed Captain and, although he had a poor series by his own standards, West Indies beat Australia for the very first time. The decision disappointed Hunte, but he played on under Sobers. Not least was this owing to Sobers being fortified and advised by Worrell, who managed the side. West Indies could now justly claim to be the best cricket team in the world; they had belief in themselves not only on the field but as citizens of the world.

Sobers, who had followed Worrell as professional at Radcliffe, regarded him as a close friend and a great captain; he had been the only West Indian in England Sobers had felt able to turn to in times of trouble. Sobers, though, did not model himself on Worrell – he never modelled himself on anyone – but Worrell helped him immeasurably, be it watching in the pavilion where Worrell could spot a player's problem before the player was aware he had one, or in conversing in the bar (Sobers, Worrell and Weekes were considered the three great drinkers of Barbados). Sobers said:

> Frank recommended me as captain because I had made suggestions to him when he was captain. He was not looking for advice but he found that some of the things I mentioned meshed with his thinking.
>
> He was a tremendous manager because he was so reliable. We discussed tactics but he did not press them on the team because he felt I had capabilities as a leader. We had one or two run-ins but they did not affect our relationship.

The two differed as captains in that Sobers led more by example than as a tactician. He did not consult others and was disadvantaged in that his career had run parallel to some of his team-mates. Worrell was an older man when he was captain. So long as Sobers was playing to the top of his form and men like Griffith, Hall and Hunte were in their prime, that was good enough; when the cracks began to show it was a different matter. Nevertheless, of that first series as captain, *Wisden* said: 'Sobers showed an instinctive tactical sense which never let him down. He was a worthy successor to Sir Frank Worrell. No higher praise can be given.'

Although after he retired Worrell was the single most influential person in West Indian cricket circles, he was never a member of West Indies Board of Control. Appointments were by nomination and he was rarely in one place long enough to be considered. It allowed him the freedom to speak his mind without having to toe an official line. In October 1966 he vehemently criticised plans to stage a match between Barbados and a Rest of the World XI. 'It is not an independence match because Barbados becomes independent on November 30 and it has been arranged for early in March,' Worrell said through the channels of the press.

> The only possible reason for this match seems to be to permit the Barbadians to prove that the Barbados team is better than West Indies. This savours of bigotry, vanity and insularity. The chambers of commerce, politicians and, indeed, all thinking West Indians see the necessity for regional co-operation. The West Indies cricket team has proved over the past six years that it is a working federal unit and for Barbados to want to prove that the part is better than the whole is a retrograde step. Of course, if this match does come off, Barbados will beat the Rest of the World team because in the Rest's team there are Englishmen who will be called to leave England in March when it is winter there. Coming to the intense glare and heat, no one can be expected to do well. . . .

Indeed, I am sure that the other players will regard this occasion as one in which they can have a darn good time at the Barbados Government's expense and could not care less whether they win, lose or draw the match.

It is also a misnomer to call the opposition the Rest of the World because one cannot have a Rest of the World team without representatives from India, Pakistan, and New Zealand. These three countries are bona fide members of the International Cricket Conference. By the same argument the South Africans should be excluded simply because they are not members of the ICC.* If the selectors wanted to get together a team which they felt was the best in the world, then they should call on the best in the world.

Worrell said that if the Barbadians wanted to prove they were a better side than the West Indies team then Gibbs, Kanhai, Butcher and Hendriks would seem to be cutting their own throats. He said the match should be cancelled as it could be the first phase in creating disunity in the ranks of West Indies cricket at a time when it was felt by all and sundry that the West Indies ranks, generally, should be firmly closed.

Three days later, having been criticised in certain quarters, Worrell apologised to Errol Barrow, Prime Minister of Barbados, and to his government for his statement. But he reiterated his opinion that the match should be cancelled. He said he had been under the impression that as it was being advertised as part of Barbados' independence celebrations, the Government would have been responsible for the cricketing guests. He wished to withdraw references to the government spending money and added that the Rest's team had nothing to gain whether they won or lost the match. The only people who stood to gain, he said, were the Barbadians. The match seemed to have been set up for the sole purpose of giving Barbados a chance of winning. It would have been better to have invited Guyana to join forces with Barbados against the Rest of West Indies.

Note
*Worrell was under a misapprehension. South Africa were still in the ICC.

13
Valediction

— ○ ○ ○ —

Established as an academic that he was, Worrell was more in demand as a lecturer than as a cricket counsellor in the last years of his life. In July 1966, while West Indies under Sobers' captaincy were again beating England in England, Worrell, who had been a tour selector, visited youth clubs and other organisations in Grenada. He received a warm welcome. As at Mona and St Augustine, he spoke of his belief in the value of physical fitness, discipline resulting from team work and possessing the right attitude towards work. Illiteracy, he said, was 'the worst of the social diseases.'

That December, at the invitation of the Government of India, Worrell left for a six-week visit to that country. As their guest he visited universities and other academic institutions, and met the All India Sports Council as well as officials of the Cricket Board of Control. He saw a considerable amount of West Indies' touring party. During the Madras Test he arrived at a dinner given by India's Board after the speeches had started, having been travelling. He was asked to speak immediately and did so with modesty, humour and sound sense. In the Calcutta Test, when the pavilion was burned down, Worrell was instrumental in persuading West Indies' team to continue playing. Some of them were scared to go back on to the field but Worrell shrugged it off. 'Riots happen the whole time,' he said.

The government felt that Worrell's visit would enhance interest in sport, particularly amongst university students and would create 'a better understanding between the people of India and West Indies'. Worrell spoke to students of their duties, obligations to themselves and their parents, to the community and to the government. He had agreed to go to India, initially, to further racial unity, at the request of Muni Lal, Indian High Commissioner in Trinidad, who was delighted with his visit. 'He inspired love and respect wherever he went,' said Lal. 'A sportsman of his stature – humble and unobtrusive – had seldom been seen on Indian campuses before. He knew neither colour nor religion and inspired all those who came into contact with him to forget these barriers.' In a special convocation ceremony in Chandigarh on 4 February 1967, the University of the Punjab conferred the honorary degree of Doctor of Law on Worrell.

Worrell, though, was not well. For perhaps the first time, he was noticeably irritable. He had not felt well enough to see Lana when he passed through England. He telephoned her and said he had sinus trouble. He constantly became tired in India, although that did not seem to show. West Indies' players, who knew him as well as most, detected no signs of ill-health. But by the end of his six-week trip he decided not to return to Trinidad, opting instead to fly to Kingston and Mona, where he was familiar with the university hospital and its staff. His intention was to have a check-up and to watch the Shell Shield match between Jamaica and Trinidad but he barely survived the journey. He insisted on calling on his old barber for a haircut but was too ill for it to be completed. He had to be taken into the hospital ward in a wheelchair. He was examined immediately by a doctor, Rolf Richards, who diagnosed leukaemia and informed the senior assistant registrar, Carl Jackman, that Worrell would not live longer than six weeks.

Jackman had the unpleasant task of contacting Velda in Trinidad and asking her to come to Jamaica without letting on how seriously ill her husband was. She was told by Richards on arrival at the airport. Worrell was not informed of the nature of his illness but they knew they could not deceive him. 'He was aware things were coming to a close,' said Ivo de Souza. Worrell told the cricket writer of Jamaica's newspaper *The Gleaner*, Strebor Roberts, that only his courage had carried him through India.

Worrell was given a blood transfusion and seemed – temporarily – to be recovering. Sometimes he would appear drowsy, at other times very ill. His condition was hardly helped when another Jamaican cricketer, Denis Thorburn, died in the same ward – also of leukaemia. It was by no means a rare disease in West Indies at the time.

Had Worrell contracted it ten years later he would have had a much better chance of living. It was, in the 1960s, a virulent illness and the variety Worrell had was particularly lethal. He remained able to be accommodating to the small number of visitors Richards permitted (a sign on the door to his ward stated 'Positively no visitors'), to apologise to his nurse for taking up her time, and to stagger out of his bed on to the balcony to gaze at the campus and the Blue Mountains. He lost 40 pounds and asked Jackman to have his clothes altered by a tailor. He sent word to Harold Brewster, requesting to have a Masonic apron brought to him. He had taken a keen interest in freemasonery late in life. He attended Lodge, the religious denomination. (Ten years before, he had been refused entry to Lodge in Barbados on account of his reputation for arrogance.) Cedric Harper, warden of Irvine, was asked to bring to the ward a photograph of Lana which was still in Worrell's old home, as were other possessions.

The night before Worrell died he was visited by Michael Clarke, who had brought into the hospital his son, suffering from meningitis, and Alf Valentine. They were told Worrell would not survive the next day; yet he was still able to speak. He died in the morning, shortly before ten o'clock, having suffered a relapse during the night. Five doctors were at his bedside. It was 13 March, only a few weeks since he had appeared to be in good health.

When the news of Worrell's death was relayed to Barbados, flags were lowered to half-mast. Tributes poured in, to the university campuses and to newspapers. By chance, the Prime Minister of Barbados, Errol Barrow, flew into Kingston on the day Worrell died, and funeral plans were swiftly arranged. It was decided Worrell would be given a state funeral in Barbados, although whether he would have chosen to be buried there is open to some doubt. Velda flew immediately to Barbados while Jackman and the Vice-Chancellor organised a memorial service at Mona and made preparations for transporting Worrell's body. Lana, now eighteen, flew out from England. A secretary had to be assigned to deal with the mound of correspondence that arrived at Mona. It came from young and old, from rich and poor, from the Queen, the Prime Minister of Jamaica, from MCC, from cricketers all over the world. The Queen said in a telegram: 'I am extremely sorry to hear of the sad death of Frank Worrell. Please convey my sympathies to his widow.'

Headley, in a message to *The Gleaner*, said that Worrell had been a brilliant cricketer of the highest standard. 'He earned a place among the game's truly greats and broke the long tradition which kept the West Indies captaincy to a special group.' Constantine, in a BBC tribute, said: 'Worrell began by being ridiculed generally and considered by most of his countrymen to be uppity. But he was a

negro with a faith in his own future who moved round the
world with a prestige and a feeling that he had a contri-
bution to make. A lot of friends were loyal to him because
he was loyal back. He was a great West Indian.' Muni Lal
wrote: 'The world is poorer today for the loss of an all-
time great cricketer and greater gentleman.' Rual Vaz, in
an interview, said: 'Worrell cherished me and I cherished
him. We developed between us a great comradeship. His
name alone, when spoken abroad, was a pass to all
respectable places as I experienced on my visit to England.
While he was in India he carried out his full series of
lectures despite his declining health. I can say that he was a
man who always lived up to his obligations.' Sobers said
that Worrell had been 'like a father to me. He has done so
much for me personally and for West Indies cricket as a
whole.' Weekes said that Worrell was probably the most
liked cricketer the Commonwealth had seen. Miller,
writing in Sydney, commented that he was 'in the Field
Marshal class. From the very first Test match in Brisbane
in 1951 when he whistled calypsos between almost every
over to the more sombre days as a critic in the press box
we became close and trusted friends.' May said that he
regarded Worrell as the most accomplished of the 'three
"W"s', and Dexter that he was one of the best captains he
had seen or played against. A lengthy obituary in *The
Times* proclaimed Worrell as being a man who not only
won personal fame but who raised the status and dignity
of the West Indian coloured cricketer.

> He himself wisely took little part in the occasionally
> acrimonious controversy over the captaincy which
> ended when he was asked to take the 1960–1 team to
> Australia. His achievement as a captain may best be
> described as instilling in his players a professional
> attitude and stability which had endured. He will be
> remembered as much for his leadership as for his play.

At Kensington Oval, the teams participating in the match between Barbados and the Rest of the World, the match that Worrell strongly criticised, stood in silence for two minutes. They were taking part in a knockout game arranged after their five-day match had ended early, the Rest having won comfortably. It was poignant that the aeroplane carrying Worrell's body should circle overhead as the Barbados team left the field. To this day Harold Brewster is convinced the timing was not coincidental.

Worrell's last resting-place was to be at Cave Hill, on a site overlooking the new university campus, three miles from his birthplace on the outskirts of Bridgetown. The majority of the West Indies players who toured under Worrell to Australia and England were at the funeral, held on 19 March. Walcott and Weekes were among the pall bearers.

At St Michael's Cathedral where the service was held and where Worrell had sung as a choir boy, all manner of persons came to pay their final respects. Jamaica was represented by its High Commissioner to Barbados, Ashton Wright, who was also a pall bearer; each West Indian government was represented. The first lesson was read by Barbados' Prime Minister – another pall bearer – and the second by Dr Hastings Huggins, Pro Vice-Chancellor of the University. The eulogy was delivered by the Revd Ivor Jones, a personal friend, who described Worrell as 'a prince among men. He simply had the stuff of which great leaders are made.' Loud-speakers relayed the service to hundreds outside; they joined in the hymn singing.

On route from cathedral to campus, past and present West Indian cricketers openly wept. The biggest crowds were in the Bank Hall area. They watched or followed the coffin on its way to Cave Hill where the Anglican Bishop of Barbados, the Rt Revd Lewis Evans, consecrated the grave before the casket draped in the gold and blue

Barbados flag with a wreath in the shape of a cricket bat laid on it was lowered beneath gloomy skies.

In Jamaica, a memorial service was held the same day in the university chapel at Mona. The Chancellor, Rual Vaz, diplomats, sportsmen, students and nurses who tended Worrell in his last days were present. One of the two lessons was read by Donald Lacy, who had been on West Indies Board when Worrell was appointed captain. The Vice-Chancellor, Sir Philip Sherlock, said in his eulogy that Worrell never did a mean thing in his words and deeds.

> He had an easy, natural generosity of spirit and was totally lacking in pomp, selfishness and self-importance. It was typical of him that he should choose to play for Boys Town instead of a more fashionable club and refuse big money offers to work on for the university.
>
> There was a quality of excellence in Sir Frank – and cricket was his medium. Even in his schooldays there had been a sense of tranquillity. And when he died, suddenly he sat up in bed and then fell back, a smile on his face.

Boys Town sent a tribute:

> The sad news of the passing of Sir Frank Worrell on Monday morning was received by members of Boys Town and the surrounding neighbourhood with profound sorrow and grief. People young and old could be seen in little groups throughout the day, some with bowed heads almost near to tears as the reality of the situation came home to them.

The tribute mentioned his leadership qualities and the benefit that had been derived by players such as Victor Fray, Gladstone Robinson and Leonard Levy. 'His demonstration of gentlemanly conduct on and off the field, patience, love, team work and understanding electrified members.'

A memorial service was also held in Norton and the following month some 1500 people including four Brewsters; the President of MCC, Britain's former Prime Minister, Sir Alec Douglas-Home; and High Commissioners from all over the world, including South Africa, attended a ceremony at Westminster Abbey. Sir Jack Hobbs had been similarly honoured at Southwark Cathedral but there had never been a service for a sportsman at Westminster Abbey. The lesson was read by Sir Lionel Luckhoo, High Commissioner for Barbados and Guyana and took in verses from the fifth chapter of St Matthew: 'How blest are the peacemakers; God shall call them his sons.' In the address which followed, E.W. Swanton, the cricket writer, said that the thought had occurred to him that no one had fulfilled those beatitudes better.

> He was essentially a bringer together by the sincerity and friendliness of his personality; a sporting catalyst in an era where international rivalries often grow sour and ugly. In the television age men famous in the world of games have a formidable influence and strange figures are sometimes magnified into heroes. Frank Worrell was the absolute antithesis of the strident and bumptious. It is his example and that of many of his West Indian playing contemporaries that has helped so much towards appreciation and admiration for his countrymen in England and throughout the Commonwealth.
>
> He was a federalist, nearest whose heart was the unity of the West Indian peoples in all their diversity. Myself, I believe he harboured a special ambition to help bring on that branch of the university in his native Barbados which is being built and on the site of which he is buried. Under the subtle knack of his personality, differences of colour and island prejudices seemed to melt away.

Swanton quoted the appreciation of an opposing captain who said of Worrell: 'However the game ended he made you feel a little better.' It was not, said Swanton, a bad epitaph. 'No doubt he made many of us feel a little better from the youngsters in Boys Town at Kingston to the Sydney "hoboes" on the hill.'

Swanton asked whether he had pictured a paragon and said that Worrell would have been horrified at the thought. 'Yet just as England brought cricket to the West Indies she, in return I believe, has given us the ideal cricketer.'

The service over – it had been relayed to the Caribbean – the muffled bells of Westminster Abbey rang out across London. Members of the congregation walked out into the spring sunshine, their thoughts far from the coming season.

In December of that same year, a fund to benefit young people in the Commonwealth and especially those attending the University of West Indies was established in memory of Worrell. Its objectives were fourfold:

1. To enable the youth of the Commonwealth countries to associate in sport and at universities of the Commonwealth and in their own country.

2. In the field of university life, to bring about a closer association between Commonwealth youth and the University of West Indies. Among other things contemplated is the offer of post-graduate UWI scholarships open to young people throughout the Commonwealth.

3. To assist sport at the University of West Indies and, more especially, to erect at its St Augustine campus a pavilion on the Frank Worrell grounds which were formally opened just a few days before his death and the laying out of which he personally directed.

4. To ensure the maintenance and education of his family.

The Duke of Norfolk chaired the United Kingdom

committee whose members included the High Commissioners in the UK for Barbados, Guyana, Jamaica, Trinidad and Tobago, and the Commissioner for the eastern Caribbean. Constantine, Dexter, May and Griffith, then secretary of MCC, served on the committee. The fund, named the Sir Frank Worrell Commonwealth Memorial Fund, was launched in June 1968. Its most ambitious aim was to provide postgraduate scholarships for young people of the United Kingdom to attend the University of West Indies. The Duke's committee also decided to attempt to collect enough money to provide an annual award in the United Kingdom for the outstanding boy cricketer of the year and to sponsor tours between English and West Indian schoolboys. In July 1970 the first of these tours took place. A team from West Indies toured England and in 1971–2 a team of English schoolboys played in the main West Indian territories. They became biennial visits and were known as the Worrell memorial tours until in 1976 the fund's resources ran out. The tours are now sponsored by Agatha Christie Ltd.

In Manchester, the West Indian Sports and Social club began raising funds to build a recreational sports centre as a memorial to Worrell. Collections, matches, a memorial service, concerts and dances were planned.

Three months after Worrell died, a conference of University of West Indies campus guild presidents established a scholarship in his memory, to be awarded to a West Indian student in social sciences.

Years after Worrell's death, his name was still being honoured. In September 1975 seven West Indian sportsmen were voted into the Black American Hall of Fame. Herb McKinley, Arthur Wint, George Headley, Garfield Sobers, Lindy Delaphena and the late Learie Constantine were the others.

In Barbados, the Ministry of Culture has, at the time of writing (1986), commissioned a life-size statue of Worrell, to be sited at the roundabout near Hall's Road, St Michael.

Velda moved from Trinidad back to Barbados and a bungalow which she had built in St Michael and named 'McGlinne' after her husband. She has not married again. She and Lana have retained their links with cricket: In 1974 Velda opened the 'three "W"s' stand at Kensington Oval after a blessing by Bishop Drexel Gomes and she still presents the Frank Worrell trophy at the conclusion of West Indies-Australia series. The Barbados Cricket Association made her a life member. Although not financially hard up by Bajan standards – Worrell had taken out insurance policies which paid for her house – the cost of living in Barbados is high. She worked as a receptionist at the Holiday Inn for six years and has taken in students. She became a director of Caribbean Airways and judged a Miss World competition in London in 1967. She receives no pension or allowance from a cricketing body or the Barbados government: Tom Adams, when he was Prime Minister, said she would be provided for but nothing came of it. Sporting heroes are transient. Her old friends, though, do not forget her. When the roof needs repairing, financial help is quickly forthcoming. Her marriage was a happy one even if Worrell did not always remain faithful to her.

Lana, having married and divorced a Jamaican, lives at the time of writing in Barbados with Clyde Walcott's son, Michael, who owns a health food store, and her child from her marriage. She works as a secretary in Bridgetown and watches Michael play weekend club cricket for Wanderers. She looks remarkably like her father and possesses similar poise and charm.

Some years after Worrell died, Gerry Alexander, who became a vet in Guyana, was in a hotel lift in India with some West Indian cricketers. An English woman got in and addressed him. 'You're from West Indies, aren't you? When I think of your country I think of Frank Worrell. Watching him play was like going to the ballet.'

Postscript by Richie Benaud

—— ○ ○ ○ ——

Frank Worrell was a great captain. I rated him especially highly because there was tremendous pressure on him to succeed in the job. He was not wanted by administrators even when given the job for the 1960–1 tour of Australia – it needed Gerry Alexander, mind you, under intense pressure from Worrell fans, to work on the West Indies Board of Control to have him installed. Had Frank failed on that tour it would have set back West Indies cricket, and especially the black cricketer, by twenty years.

Captaining Australia against his side that series, I saw for the first time that West Indies had been moulded into a team. Frank was a good tactician with a very calm exterior that showed particularly at Brisbane and Melbourne. But his greatest ability was that he led his players as would a father. He had a calm influence on excitable individuals like Rohan Kanhai and Gary Sobers, and every player worshipped him. They did exactly what he asked of them. He and I had chatted beforehand about the series we might have and it was, in fact, a fluke that it turned out so well. West Indies had a very ordinary tour leading up to the first Test. It was because of Frank they never collapsed when the tension mounted, as had been their wont in the past. They did much for our cricket in Australia.

I never detected any resentment from Frank that he did not gain the captaincy earlier. There was perhaps a calm shaking of the head as if to say, why are people so stupid? Headley and Walcott or Weekes should have captained West Indies – it was ridiculous that Denis Atkinson, fine character that he was, was appointed before the 'three "W"'s' during that 1955 tour. However, in my opinion, no one else but Frank could have turned West Indies from being the most brilliant bunch of individual cricketers in the world into a close-knit team. Clive Lloyd has built on what he achieved, bringing even more professional composure to excitable play. Frank, though, did it in his very first series as captain which was a magnificent achievement.

Statistics

compiled by Simon Wilde

First-Class Cricket (1941–64)

Table 1

Season	Matches	Innings	Not Outs	Runs	Highest Innings	100s	Av.
1941–2	2	4	1	70	34*	–	23.33
1942–3	4	7	2	386	188	1	77.20
1943–4	2	3	1	347	308*	1	173.50
1944–5	4	7	0	325	113	1	46.43
1945–6	1	2	1	271	255*	1	271.00
1946–7	2	4	1	148	67*	–	49.33
1947–8	7	10	4	568	131*	2	94.67
1949–50 (India, Pakistan and Ceylon)	17	26	4	1640	223*	5	74.55
1950	22	31	5	1775	261	6	68.27
1950–1 (India and Ceylon)	22	33	3	1900	285	5	63.33
1951	2	3	0	88	52	–	29.33
1951–2 (Australia and New Zealand)	12	22	4	872	160*	3	48.44
1952	1	2	0	97	62	–	48.50
1952–3	6	10	1	446	237	1	49.56
1953	2	4	0	83	37	–	20.75
1953–4 (India)	11	16	0	833	165	4	52.06
1953–4	4	8	1	334	167	1	47.71

Table 1 *(continued)*

Season	Matches	Innings	Not Outs	Runs	Highest Innings	100s	Av.
1954	2	3	1	116	74	–	58.00
1954–5	7	13	0	378	100	1	29.08
1955	2	4	0	178	100	1	44.50
1957	20	34	9	1470	191*	4	58.80
1958	2	3	0	173	101	1	57.67
1959	1	2	0	79	54	–	39.50
1959–60	5	7	1	395	197*	1	65.83
1960–1 (Australia)	12	22	3	818	82	–	43.05
1961	2	3	0	46	29	–	15.33
1961–2	6	8	3	403	98*	–	80.60
1963	18	23	2	522	74*	–	24.86
1963–4	5	6	1	158	73	–	31.60
1964	5	6	1	106	42	–	21.20
Totals	208	326	49	15025	308*	39	54.24

*signifies not out or unbroken partnership

Worrell also took in first-class cricket 349 wickets at 28.98 each and 139 catches.

In Table 1 Worrell was playing in either West Indies or England unless stated. He played for Barbados from 1941–2 to 1946–7 and Jamaica from 1947–8 to 1963–4. He toured with West Indies in 1950, 1951–2, 1957, 1960–1 and 1963 and with the Commonwealth XI in 1949–50, 1950–1 and 1953–4. He also played in England for the Commonwealth XI (1951–5, 1958), A.E.R. Gilligan's XI (1958–9), MCC (1961, 1964), Free Foresters (1964) and Sir Frank Worrell's West Indian XI (1964).

Table 2 Summary

Country	Matches	Innings	Not Outs	Runs	Highest Innings	100s	Av.
Australia	21	39	5	1437	160*	2	42.27
Ceylon	4	6	1	494	285	1	98.80
England	79	118	18	4733	261	12	47.33
India	44	66	6	3840	223*	13	64.00
New Zealand	3	5	2	253	100	1	84.33
Pakistan	2	3	0	39	17	–	13.00
West Indies	55	89	17	4229	308*	10	58.74
Totals	208	326	49	15025	308*	39	54.24

*signifies not out or unbroken partnership

Table 3 Centuries

188	Barbados v Trinidad, Port of Spain, 1942–3
308*	Barbados v Trinidad, Bridgetown, 1943–4
113	Barbados v Trinidad, Port of Spain, 1944–5
255*	Barbados v Trinidad, Port of Spain, 1945–6
131*	West Indies v England, Georgetown, 1947–8
106*	Jamaica v MCC, Melbourne Park, Kingston, 1947–8
109	Commonwealth XI v Indian Universities, Bombay, 1949–50
154	Commonwealth XI v North Zone, Patiala, 1949–50
165	Commonwealth XI v West Zone, Poona, 1949–50
223*	Commonwealth XI v India, Kanpur, 1949–50
161	Commonwealth XI v India, Madras, 1949–50
160	West Indians v Cambridge University, Fenner's, 1950
104	West Indians v Somerset, Taunton, 1950
159	West Indians v Lancashire, Liverpool, 1950
241*	West Indians v Leicestershire, Leicester, 1950
261	West Indies v England, Trent Bridge, 1950
138	West Indies v England, Oval, 1950
127	Commonwealth XI v Raja of Jath's XI, Poona, 1950–1
116	Commonwealth XI v Bihar Governor's XI, Jamshedpur, 1950–1
102	Commonwealth XI v Hyderabad State XI, Hyderabad, 1950–1
116	Commonwealth XI v India, Kanpur, 1950–1
285	Commonwealth XI v Ceylon, Colombo, 1950–1
108	West Indies v Australia, Melbourne, 1951–2
160*	West Indians v Tasmania, Hobart, 1951–2
100	West Indies v New Zealand, Auckland, 1951–2
237	West Indies v India, Sabina Park, Kingston, 1952–3
104	Commonwealth XI v Baroda, Baroda, 1953–4
143	Commonwealth XI v Indian XI, Ahmedabad, 1953–4
110	Commonwealth XI v North Zone, Amritsar, 1953–4
165	Commonwealth XI v Indian XI, Nagpur, 1953–4

Table 3 *(continued)*

167   West Indies v England, Port of Spain, 1953–4
100   Jamaica v Trinidad, Sabina Park, Kingston, 1954–5
100   Commonwealth XI v England XI, Torquay, 1955
107*   West Indians v Northamptonshire, Northampton, 1957
135   West Indians v Sussex, Hove, 1957
191*   West Indies v England, Trent Bridge, 1957
104   West Indians v Leicestershire, Leicester, 1957
101   A.E.R. Gilligan's XI v New Zealanders, Hastings, 1958
197*   West Indies v England, Bridgetown, 1959–60

Table 4 Six or more Wickets in an Innings

7–70   West Indies v England, Headingley, 1957
6–38   West Indies v Australia, Adelaide, 1951–2
6–71   West Indians v MCC, Lord's, 1957

Test Cricket

Table 1

Season	Opponents	Matches	Innings	Not Outs	Runs	Highest Innings	100s	Av.
1947–8	England	3	4	2	294	131*	1	147.00
1950	England	4	6	0	539	261	2	89.83
1951–2	Australia	5	10	0	337	108	1	33.70
1951–2	N. Zealand	2	3	1	233	100	1	116.50
1952–3	India	5	8	0	398	237	1	49.75
1953–4	England	4	8	1	334	167	1	47.71
1954–5	Australia	4	8	0	206	61	–	25.75
1957	England	5	10	1	350	191*	1	38.89
1959–60	England	4	6	1	320	197*	1	64.00
1960–1	Australia	5	10	0	375	82	–	37.50
1961–2	India	5	6	2	332	98*	–	83.00
1963	England	5	8	1	142	74*	–	20.29
Totals		51	87	9	3860	261	9	49.49

*signifies not out or unbroken partnership

Worrell also took in Test cricket 69 wickets at 38.73 each and 43 catches.

Table 2 Summary

Opponents	Matches	Innings	Not Outs	Runs	Highest Innings	100s	Average
Australia	14	28	0	918	108	1	32.79
England	25	42	6	1979	261	6	54.97
India	10	14	2	730	237	1	60.83
New Zealand	2	3	1	233	100	1	116.50
Totals	51	87	9	3860	261	9	49.49

Worrell is the only batsman to have shared in two partnerships of over 500 runs in first-class cricket. He added 502 unbroken with J.D.C. Goddard for the fourth wicket for Barbados v Trinidad at Bridgetown in 1943–4, which was at the time a world fourth-wicket record. That was subsequently beaten when Worrell and C.L. Walcott added 574 unbroken (in 335 minutes) for Barbados v Trinidad at Port of Spain in 1945–6, a stand which established a new record for any wicket in first-class cricket. This was surpassed thirteen months later when Vijay S. Hazare and Gul Mahomed put on 577 for Baroda's fourth wicket against Holkar at Baroda, but it has not been beaten since.

Other major stands in which Worrell has shared:
399　4th wkt　with G.S. Sobers, West Indies v England,
　　　　　　　　Bridgetown, 1959–60 (West Indies
　　　　　　　　Test record for the fourth wicket)
350　3rd wkt　with E.D. Weekes, West Indians v
　　　　　　　　Cambridge University, Fenner's, 1950
340*　3rd wkt　with E.D. Weekes, West Indians v
　　　　　　　　Leicestershire, Leicester, 1950
338　3rd wkt　with E.D. Weekes, West Indies v England,
　　　　　　　　Port of Spain, 1953–4 (West Indies
　　　　　　　　Test record for the third wicket)
301　5th wkt　with W.H.H. Sutcliffe, Commonwealth
　　　　　　　　XI v Ceylon, Colombo, 1950–1

283   4th wkt   with E.D. Weekes, West Indies v England,
                 Trent Bridge, 1950
281   2nd wkt   with C.L. Walcott, West Indians v
                 Tasmania, Hobart, 1951–2
98*   10th wkt   with W.W. Hall, West Indies v India, Port
                 of Spain, 1961–2 (West Indies Test
                 record for the tenth wicket)

The partnership with Sobers (above) lasted 570 minutes and provides the only instance in Test cricket of two batsmen staying together throughout two consecutive days of play. Worrell's innings of 197* in 682 minutes is the longest for West Indies in Test cricket.

During his innings of 261 for West Indies v England at Trent Bridge in 1950, Worrell scored 239 runs in a day (0* to 239* on the second day), a West Indies Test record, and in all 152 runs in boundaries (two sixes and 35 fours). His previous first-class innings had been 241* for West Indians v Leicestershire at Leicester.

Worrell's aggregate of 1900 runs in India and Ceylon in 1950–1 was a record for a non-English season of first-class cricket until beaten by J.R. Reid's total of 2188 runs in South Africa and Australasia in 1961–2.

Worrell carried his bat through a completed innings of 372 for 191* for West Indies v England at Trent Bridge in 1957, when he was on the field for the first 20½ hours of the match.

In his first Test match, against England at Port of Spain in 1947–8, Worrell scored 97 and 28*, and in his second, at Georgetown in the same series, he scored 131*.

Worrell's innings for 110 for the Commonwealth XI v North Zone at Amritsar in 1953–4 was completed before lunch on the first day of the match.

Worrell did not fail to score in any of his first 31 Test matches, but was subsequently dismissed for a duck 11

*signifies not out or unbroken partnership

times in Test cricket, including eight times against England. He was dismissed for a pair against Australia at Melbourne in 1960–1.

Worrell captained West Indies in 15 Tests, from 1960–1 to 1963, winning nine, losing three, drawing two, with the match against Australia at Brisbane in 1960–1 ending in a tie, the only tie in Test cricket. He led West Indies to a five–nil win in the series against India in West Indies in 1961–2, one of only five instances of a side winning all five Tests of a rubber.

League cricket, compiled by Colin Atkin

Table 1 Radcliffe 1948–53; Norton 1956, 1958, 1959

Season	Innings	Not outs	Runs	Highest score	Average
1948	22	7	773	123*	51.53
1949	27	10	1501	150*	88.29
1951	25	10	1694	146*	112.80
1952	24	10	1082	152*	77.28
1953	23	7	1326	117*	82.87
1956	18	6	711	100	59.02
1958	21	8	1002	132*	77.01
1959	21	5	1014	116*	63.04
Totals	101	63	9103	152	77.14

Table 2 Bowling

Season	Overs	Maidens	Runs	Wickets	Av.	5 wkts	Posn in League Averages
1948	252.5	44	761	58	13.12	5	10th
1949	312.6	45	1068	66	16.18	3	17th
1950	8	–	42	1	42.00	–	–
1951	263.3	21	1182	72	15.57	4	18th
1952	296	53	872	72	12.11	6	16th
1953	448	75	1269	93	13.64	11	15th

Worrell took 5 more wickets in a match on thirty occasions – most in a season, 11 in 1953.

In all, Worrell took 382 wickets – his best season being 1953 when he took 93 wickets.

Worrell's best bowling performance was 8 wickets for 34 runs against Stockport on 14 July 1953.

Worrell took 54 catches in all – his best season being 1952, when he took 15 catches.

On 4 August 1951 Worrell surpassed his own Central Lancashire League record of 1501 runs that he set in 1949. He scored, in the 1951 season, 1694 runs. His average of 112.80 beat the previous best, 100.84 by Leslie Warburton in 1937. Worrell reached 1000 runs on 30 June which was the quickest achievement for the Central Lancashire League.

In 1950, when he was touring England with West Indies, Worrell played in one match for Radcliffe as deputy professional, on 5 August. The match was against Rochdale at Radcliffe. Worrell scored 10 runs and took 1 for 42.

In 1954, Worrell acted as deputy professional for Heywood. He scored 44 not out and took 3 for 39. In 1956 he acted as deputy professional for Oldham. In five innings he made 80 runs with a highest score of 35 not out. He took 17 wickets for 239 and held 2 catches.

Worrell was involved in eleven century partnerships during his five seasons at Radcliffe, the best of which was against Middleton on 31 May 1952 when he and W. Greenhalgh scored 303 for the first wicket. This was a record for the Central Lancashire League and one which still stands at the time of writing, 1985, as does Worrell's aggregate for 1951. He scored a half-century at least once on every ground in the Central Lancashire League, 27 being made on Radcliffe's ground.

In 1961, Worrell acted as deputy professional for Church in the Lancashire League when C. Watson was involved in a car accident. Worrell played against Enfield on 1 July and, having been dropped in the slips on 1, went on to make 105 not out in a total of 168. He took 1 wicket for 41.

Index